The Pursuit of
the Presidency

The Pursuit of the Presidency

'92 and Beyond

by Christine M. Black

Oryx Press
1994

The rare Arabian Oryx is believed to have inspired the myth of the unicorn. This desert antelope became virtually extinct in the early 1960s. At that time several groups of international conservationists arranged to have 9 animals sent to the Phoenix Zoo to be the nucleus of a captive breeding herd. Today the Oryx population is over 800, and nearly 400 have been returned to reserves in the Middle East.

Copyright © 1994 by The Oryx Press
4041 North Central at Indian School Road
Phoenix, Arizona 85012-3397

Cover photo by Wendy Maeda, *Boston Globe*

Published simultaneously in Canada

Printed and Bound in the United States of America

∞ The paper used in this publication meets the minimum requirements of American National Standard for Information Science—Permanence of Paper for Printed Library Materials, ANSI Z39.48,1984.

Library of Congress Cataloging-in-Publication Data
Black, Christine M.
    The pursuit of the presidency : '92 and beyond / by Christine M. Black.
      p. cm.
    Includes bibliographical references and index.
    ISBN 0-89774-845-X
    1. Presidents—United States—Election—1992. 2. Presidents—United States—Election. I. Title.
    E884.B57 1994   93-37593
    324.973'0928—dc20   CIP

Contents

Preface

To the uninitiated, the rules and rituals of politics can be as strange and offputting as the customs and practices of an alien culture. Electoral politics, in particular, seems to have become an insiders' game with little relevance to real people and real lives. Many young people find politics and government confusing or boring or both.

The purpose of this book is to draw back the curtain and show, in a way that is clear and compelling, the inner workings of a political campaign and how a campaign relates to the business of governing. This book is intended to be a road map that carries readers across the geographic sweep of the United States during the presidential election of 1992. Politics is nothing like the dry and dusty stuff of a bad civics class. In fact, nothing is more fascinating than the pursuit of power in a democracy. A campaign is about real people, real issues, and real emotions. It is about wildly euphoric successes and deeply depressing losses. It is about passion and promise, daring and deceit, ambition and commitment. There is a direct connection between the outcome of an election and the environmental standards of the nation, the enforcement of civil rights, the level of taxation, and the quality of public services. Politics matters.

Only one president of the United States, George Washington, the nation's first chief executive, was picked by acclamation. It has been necessary for the others to seek and secure support by campaigning for the office. During the more than 200-year history of this republic, campaigns have evolved and changed. This book traces the evolution of the presidential primary, the change in the role of nominating conventions, and the growing reliance on technological innovations such as television in modern presidential campaigns. It discusses in detail the new ways in which candidates used television and radio to communicate directly with voters in 1992.

For young people, the 1992 campaign has special meaning. While Bill Clinton, the candidate who won, is old enough to be the father of many of the readers of this book, he represents a new, energetic generation coming to power. Just as young people were inspired by John Kennedy's election in 1960, so young people today should be able to recognize their own promise and future in Clinton's success in 1992.

A number of recent studies have found a distressing level of political illiteracy in young people. This book is a primer especially for them, but it is also for all Americans, to help show that politics is interesting, fun, and important to their lives. The material from this book is drawn from personal observation during the 1992 campaign and more than 20 years of experience as a political reporter.

Introduction

Those of us who cover presidential campaigns admit to being hardcore junkies who can never get enough of politics. We find the pursuit of the presidency not only an endlessly interesting exercise in democracy but also a unique window into United States' culture. Many people think that politics is confusing and irrelevant. The 1992 campaign provided persuasive evidence to the contrary. Thanks to a roused electorate, the 1992 campaign had clarity, focus, and relevance. A new generation seized power, millions of citizens became political activists for the first time, and methods for communicating with voters improved and expanded.

My first out-of-town 1992 presidential campaign assignment for the *Boston Globe* was Bill Clinton's announcement of candidacy in October of 1991 in Little Rock. My last assignment for this campaign was his inauguration in Washington in January of 1993. In between the Clinton bookends, I covered some of the best stories of the year, including Pat Buchanan's Republican insurgency, Jerry Brown's political movement, Clinton's climb back into public favor in June, and Ross Perot's second coming in October as well as the Democratic and Republican nominating conventions and the presidential debates.

When my friend and colleague, Thomas Oliphant, a *Globe* political columnist, and I wrote *All By Myself*, a book on the 1988 campaign, we argued that the nation wanted change and might have voted for Democratic nominee Michael Dukakis had he been able to articulate a compelling vision for the future. We found the outlines of a future Democratic victory in Dukakis' loss. Hindsight also makes it clear that in 1988 George Bush sowed the seeds of his eventual defeat by running a negative and personalized campaign that failed to address the real concerns of voters. The seeds sprouted and grew into weeds that choked his reelection campaign in 1992.

The 1992 campaign heartened those of us sitting at the back of the campaign plane because voters paid close attention and demanded real answers from these presidential hopefuls. The candidates whom I call the truth tellers—Paul Tsongas, Pat Buchanan, Jerry Brown, and Ross Perot—may not have won the election but each left deep footprints on the process and on the man who is now president of the United States. In this book I try not only to tell a terrific story about an exciting campaign but also explain how Clinton won and Bush lost and give some insight into the inner workings of a presidential campaign.

I was a 20-year-old trainee reporter at *The Sun*, the daily newspaper in Lowell, Massachusetts, when I interviewed my first presidential candidate, Senator George S. McGovern of South Dakota. He was well on his way to winning the Democratic presidential nomination when I spoke to him on a drive from Lawrence to Lowell while he was campaigning for votes in the Massachusetts primary. I was nervous and ran out of questions before we arrived at 15 Kearney Square in downtown Lowell. But Senator McGovern was gracious, even if puzzled by the unusual youth of this campaign reporter who was not yet old enough to vote. (The voting age had not yet been lowered from 21 to 18.) Twenty years and five presidential campaigns later, I no longer get flustered by candidates, but I remain awed and excited by the resilience and strength of the democratic process.

Most of the material in this book came directly from my own files and notebooks from this campaign. For those interested in a more in-depth look at the modern presidential selection process, there are many other books to consult, beginning with the *Making of the President* series written by the late Theodore White. My friends and colleagues, Jack Germond and Jules Witcover, write a compelling account of the campaign every four years.

Special thanks to my newspaper and television friends from the campaign trail, especially Gabriel Stix of CBS News, to the *Boston Globe* which sends me out to cover the political wars every four years, and to the news organizations and photographers who granted permission to use the photographs that appear in this book. Thanks to Dan Wasserman, the *Globe*'s talented cartoonist whose brilliantly funny cartoons tell the story so much better than my paltry words. Particular thanks to Sean Mullin and Bob Yaeger, the Globe computer geniuses who helped this technophobe get her manuscript computer-ready, and the *Globe* staff photographers, especially John Tlumacki who provided his fabulous inauguration pictures for this book.

Chris Black
Boston, Massachusetts
August 1993

The Pursuit of
the Presidency

Chapter 1

The Torch Is Passed: Bill Clinton Assumes the Presidency

THE INAUGURATION

The enormous crowd gathered before the U.S. Capitol suddenly stirred, like some sort of primordial beast roused from a slumber, and began a lazy roll towards the sidewalks of Pennsylvania Avenue to watch the inaugural parade on January 20, 1993. No one rushed, pushed, or panicked despite the crush of humanity. Strangers smiled at one another. The subway was so jammed that thousands decided to walk to the celebratory parties being held in swank business offices and fancy hotel meeting rooms lining the parade route.

The inaugural ceremony itself had only taken minutes. At noon, George Herbert Walker Bush still held the position of president of the United States, the highest office in the land. Not 15 minutes later, William Jefferson Clinton, a man young enough to be his son, took his place, swore to uphold the U.S. Constitution, and spoke his first words as the nation's 42nd president. Not since John F. Kennedy replaced Dwight D. Eisenhower 32 years earlier had the torch of leadership been passed to a new generation.

Hundreds of thousands of fellow citizens—Hollywood stars, U.S. Senators, old friends from Clinton's home state of Arkan-

Bill Clinton swears to uphold the U.S. Constitution while standing between his daughter Chelsea (left) and wife Hillary (right). (Photo by John Tlumacki, *Boston Globe*.)

sas, and rabid Democrats who just could not bear to miss this moment when a Democrat took back the presidency—attended the ceremony on that crisp and sunny winter day. Millions more all over the world watched on television. Clinton's wife, Hillary Rodham Clinton, a lawyer who epitomized the changes that had taken place in women's lives in the past 32 years, held a Clinton family Bible on which her husband swore the oath of office. A few minutes later, a green Marine Corps helicopter lifted off from behind the imposing Capitol dome and carried away former President Bush and his wife Barbara. People in the crowd cheerfully waved good-bye as the Bush's began the trip to their adopted home of Houston, Texas, to begin a new life in retirement, what Bush jokingly called "the grandchild business."

The speed and simplicity of the inaugural ceremony—its very normalcy—belied its significance. In many countries, power is held and transferred only by force. The person with a gun is the person in charge. But every four years, the oldest democracy in the world, the United States of America, reaffirms the majesty and magic of selfgovernment with the orderly and peaceful transfer of power.

"Today," said Clinton stirred by the deep meaning of these moments, "we celebrate the mystery of American renewal." The new young president made a gracious bow to the past and saluted the generation of his parents, George Bush's generation, for their contributions to the country. He then looked to the present and spoke of the generational responsibility to nurture democracy. "Each generation of Americans must define what it means to be an American," he said. He talked about the future and the need to break America of the bad habit of expecting something for nothing. He praised voters for voting for change and "forcing the spring," a new beginning for the country. Then with strength and conviction ringing in his voice, he said, "Well, my fellow Americans, this is our time. Let us embrace it." To drive home the point, he gave the word "our" an extra punch of passion and energy.

BILL CLINTON

The 46-year-old Bill Clinton was the first member of his generation, the baby boom generation born after the end of World War II, to become president. At this moment, he realized a goal that first began to form 30 years earlier when he was a high school boy in Hot Springs, Arkansas. Clinton had been a bright boy with a

President Bush leaves Washington in the presidential helicopter as an average citizen for the first time in 12 years at the Clinton inauguration. (Photo by John Tlumacki, *Boston Globe.*)

Clinton embraces his wife and daughter just minutes after becoming the 42nd president of the United States. (Photo by John Tlumacki, *Boston Globe*.)

precocious bent for politics. He won an election at the age of 16 to represent his home state in Washington in the American Legion's Boys State program, a program that introduces young people to the democratic political process and the U.S. government. That year, the Boys State participants met President Kennedy in the Rose Garden of the White House, and Clinton shook hands with the president. The brief meeting had been captured on film that a Clinton campaign consultant discovered in 1992 on a hunt through the archives at the Kennedy Presidential Library in Dorchester, Massachusetts. The grainy black-and-white segment of film was used in a campaign biography of Clinton.

In the campaign commercial, the film was deliberately slowed at the moment when an excited, teenaged Clinton reaches out to shake the hand of his hero. The slow motion picture of two hands touching underscored a symbolic continuum of leadership between two Democrats, one long dead, the other very much alive.

Kennedy and Clinton

In many ways, Kennedy and Clinton were very different. Kennedy had been the son of a wealthy and successful Boston businessman. His father's dreams drove his pursuit of power. Joseph P. Kennedy was the son of Irish Catholic immigrants who used the political successes of his sons to win acceptance from the powerful elite of white Anglo-Saxon Protestants who controlled the financial and governmental establishment of his time. By contrast, Clinton was born to a poor, widowed mother in the tiny town of Hope, Arkansas, just months after his father died in a car crash. He worked his own way to the pinnacles of power. His drive to succeed came from within. He, rather than Kennedy, more closely represented the classic American success story of a poor child who achieves fame and honor because of grit and talent, drive and determination.

Although they traveled to the presidency from starkly different starting points, there were still striking similarities between the two men and their place in American history. President Kennedy, like Clinton, was a youthful representative of a new generation moving to power. Kennedy had been the first U.S. president born in the twentieth century and the first member of his generation—the generation that survived the Great Depression in the 1930s, fought World War II in the 1940s, and built the postwar prosperity in the 1950s—to seize the reins of presidential power. Kennedy had inspired a generation of young Americans with his charm and dazzle and call to public service. Both were Democrats who believed in using government to better the lives of average people. The day before Clinton took on the awesome responsibilities of the presidency, he visited John Kennedy's grave at nearby Arlington National Ceremony with members of the Kennedy family. He often said that he wanted to emulate the president who had been killed by an assassin's bullet before realizing his own promise. Clinton also wanted to inspire young people as Kennedy had.

THE FIRST HOURS OF THE CLINTON PRESIDENCY

The inauguration on January 20, 1993, also signaled the end of the 1992 presidential campaign. A political campaign is a struggle

Fireworks illuminated the sky over the reflecting pond and the Lincoln Memorial at one of the many open-to-the-public events celebrating Clinton's inauguration. (Photo by John Tlumacki, *Boston Globe.*)

to capture the minds and hearts of a plurality of voting Americans in order to set the policy and introduce the programs to guide the nation for a four-year term. Within 48 hours of becoming president, Clinton used his new power and authority to change policies and practices of the Reagan and Bush presidencies. With a flick of the presidential pen, he abolished the White House Competitiveness Council. Presidents Reagan and Bush said that the council was supposed to cut through excessive regulation that strangled business. But Clinton's vice president, Albert Gore, Jr., a U.S. senator from Tennessee and an environmental advocate, charged that the Competitiveness Council had given big business a way to circumvent federal government environmental rules and regulations. So when Clinton and Gore took over, they locked and barred what Gore called a back door into the White House.

Abortion

With another flick of the pen, Clinton lifted restrictions on abortion counseling, fetal tissue research, and abortion in overseas military hospitals. The platform, or statement of principles, of the Republican party advocated a Constitutional amendment that would outlaw abortion. The Democratic party platform and Clinton wanted to keep abortion legal. During the Reagan and Bush administrations, anti-abortion activists had successfully prodded the Republican presidents to impose restrictions upon abortion. Federal regulation forbade doctors and nurses in federally assisted family planning clinics from telling their pregnant patients about how they might end a pregnancy through abortion. Another regulation prohibited the U.S. military from providing abortion services overseas, and a third withheld federal money from experimentation that used tissue from aborted fetuses to treat a number of diseases, including illnesses that caused premature deterioration of the brain cells. Opponents to abortion could not outlaw abortion because an earlier Supreme Court ruling that made the medical procedure legal was still in effect. But they could and did use their political influence in the Reagan and Bush administrations to chip away at abortion rights by making it more difficult for women to obtain safe and legal abortions.

The issue of abortion had sharply divided the American people. Opponents of abortion rights considered abortion akin to murder. Supporters of abortion rights viewed it was a critical civil right for women to decide when to have a baby. Many people had mixed feelings: They were uncomfortable with the notion of women using abortion as a method of birth control, but a clear majority wanted to keep abortion legal. Candidate Clinton had promised to remove restrictions on the right to abortion, and President Clinton delivered on his promise by reversing policies that had been in effect for the past 12 years.

Homosexuals in the Military

Clinton also said he intended to keep his promise and lift the ban that prevented homosexuals from serving in the military. That issue dominated his first week in office as military officers and conservative Christian groups expressed outrage that this president would keep this promise. The issue refused to die. The controversy raged throughout the first months of Clinton's administration. Clinton found a particularly stubborn adversary in a fellow Democrat, Senator Sam Nunn of Georgia, chairman of the Senate Armed Services Committee. Because of Nunn's opposition and the toll the controversy took on Clinton's popularity, Clinton finally prepared to compromise. The "don't ask, don't tell" compromise would end the military policy of asking the sexual orientation of recruits and military service members and end the practice of searching out homosexuals in the military. But gay rights groups bitterly complained that it fell short of guaranteeing civil rights to homosexuals who served in the armed forces.

THE 1992 PRESIDENTIAL CAMPAIGN

The purpose and meaning of the astonishing political campaign of 1992 had not always been clear. The campaign of 1992 was one in which the conventional wisdom as preached by the pundits who live within the confines of the Washington Beltway, the highway that spans the capital city, was almost always wrong. The only thing that could be counted upon during the turbulent year was that the unexpected would happen. And it did, over and over again. A third party candidate, H. Ross Perot, a Texas billionaire who had never held public office, ran for president and won an amazing 19 percent of the vote. The incumbent president whom all the polls and pundits said was almost unbeatable after the Persian Gulf War in 1990 was challenged by a member of his own party for his party nomination and never caught his stride as a campaigner. None of the well-known and established Democratic office holders wanted to take the chance and run against Bush who saw his popularity zoom to record highs after the Gulf War, and so it fell to the younger and less well-known Democrats to challenge the sitting president.

During the nominating season, the Democratic front-runner seemed to change every Tuesday with the results of another primary or caucus contest. Clinton emerged as the victor only after a prolonged fight. From a political standpoint, he was a bloody and scarred winner because serious questions had been raised about his character and his record as governor of one of the nation's poorest states. By June, he ran third in public opinion polls behind both Bush and Perot, and even some Democrats thought he could never win the election in November.

Issues of Personality, Style, and Character

Political campaigns in the United States turn as often on the vagaries of personality, style, and character as they do on issues of abortion rights or taxation policy. Unlike countries that have parliamentary systems of government, the United States' political parties are sometimes hard to tell apart. In parliamentary systems, the political party platforms are more important than the personalities of the politicians. A prime minister is elected by peers in the parliament, not directly by the people, so a party's ability to win seats is more important than a candidate's personal appeal to voters. The U.S. system with the direct election of a president can often be diverted by issues that seem unimportant in the long run but assume major importance at the time. In 1992, these personal issues included Hillary Rodham Clinton's influence and role in her husband's campaign, Clinton's alleged infidelity and his attempts to smoke marijuana and avoid the draft when he was a student, and Vice President Dan Quayle's criticism of a situation comedy character, Murphy Brown, for having a child out of wedlock and his inability to correctly spell potato.

The Year of the Voter

By 1992, voters had become increasingly disenchanted with politics and disengaged from their government. Many felt that the wealthy and special interests controlled the government, which is supposed to be of, by, and for the people. In 1988, after a sorry presidential campaign in which symbols such as the American flag received more attention than substantive issues such as the growing crisis in health care coverage, the lowest number of Americans in history, less than 50 percent, bothered to go to the polls to vote in the presidential election. The low level of voter participation sent an ominous signal. The United States government is a representative democracy in which a majority of voting adults select people who share their point of view to represent them at each level of government. The success of a representative democracy is dependent upon an informed and involved electorate. Voters have a responsibility to learn what they can about the candidates and issues and to vote. If they relinquish that role and responsibility, then the small number of people who do participate get control of the government, and it is no longer representative of a majority of people and instead represents the narrow special interests that finance the political campaigns.

But 1992 was the year in which people took back their government. During his inaugural address, Clinton challenged the Congress to join him in reforming government and campaign finance. "Let us reform our politics so that power and privilege no longer shout down the voice of the people," he said. "Let us give this capital back to the people to whom it belongs." The very fact that Clinton was speaking these words at that moment spoke to his success in reaching people and acting as their advocate during his campaign. Candidates who connected with voters did so by introducing innovations to their campaigns such as toll-free telephone numbers that allowed voters to call them with suggestions or complaints or campaign contributions. Television, a medium that some had blamed for creating distance between the populace and politicians, and talk radio became ways to restore intimacy to the relationship and rebuild trust between voters and those who wanted to represent them in Washington.

The Economy and the Election

By 1992 President Bush was in political trouble because the economy had been undergoing major changes for more than ten years. The economic statistics told the story. Since the election of Ronald Reagan, a Republican president, in 1980, the United States had gone from being a creditor nation that sold more of its goods than it purchased from foreign countries to a debtor nation that bought more than it sold. The national debt and the federal deficit had grown to the highest level in history, and the decline in manufacturing jobs, the well paying factory jobs that had helped create a large and prosperous middle class, had fallen so markedly that the middle class itself felt pinched and endangered. The pollsters who were measuring public opinion found that a majority of voters thought the country was going in the wrong direction and felt pessimistic about the future, a startling attitude for a country built on the belief that tomorrow would always be better.

Bush preferred international relations—meeting with foreign heads of state and lining up allies to meet world crises—to figuring out how to reform the U.S. health care system or change the welfare system. He found international diplomacy and meeting the challenges of foreign policy more satisfying than domestic affairs and dealing with members of the overwhelmingly Democratic Congress. Bush spent more time traveling overseas than any other president in history. Great changes had taken place in the world during his time in office. The Berlin Wall, that barrier between East and West Berlin that represented a physical wall between communism and democracy, had literally come down at the end of 1989, and with astonishing rapidity, East and West Germany, divided after World War II, began to reunite. The communist regimes in Eastern Europe and the Soviet Union began to break apart, and the separate nations that were brought together under the flag of communism, discarded the communist system and declared independence. Bush also presided over the brief Persian Gulf War, which wiped out once and for all the United States feeling of inadequacy in military affairs that had lingered since Vietnam fell beneath the influence of the communists in the mid-1970s.

Bush and the Republicans pointed with pride to these dramatic changes in the world. While most Americans agreed that the changes were wonderful, many were deeply distressed about the economy at home and feared that they might not have jobs unless government policies changed. When the economy is bad, the party and person in power gets blamed. From Patrick J. Buchanan, Bush's Republican challenger, whose slogan was "America First," to Jerry Brown, a Democratic presidential candidate who urged voters to take back their country, the candidates for president in 1992 exploited these concerns.

Political Cycles

Bush was also in trouble because he was a Republican president at a time political scientists were predicting that the United States was ending a conservative cycle and moving into a more progressive and populist time. While it was sometimes difficult to discern substantive differences between Democrats and Republicans, the Democratic party had become viewed as the party of liberals and more activist government, while the Republican party was the party of the conservatives and a philosophy of small government. In American history, there tended to be decades of liberal or progressive politics followed by more conservative times. A conservative era seemed to trigger a liberal reaction and vice versa.

The Democratic Challenger

It was against this backdrop that Clinton announced his candidacy in October 1991 in Little Rock, Arkansas, the poor and rural state where he had served as governor for 12 years. Clinton had been the youngest governor in the country when first elected at the age of 32. He lost his first campaign for reelection but came back two years later to serve for ten more years until he had become the most senior governor in the country. His political party, the Democratic party, the oldest political party in the nation, had not fared well in presidential politics during his years in political life. Except for one brief term of Jimmy Carter, the former governor of Georgia who captured the presidency in 1976 by running against the federal government as a Washington outsider, the Republican party had controlled the White House since Richard M. Nixon won the 1968 campaign by promising to end the still escalating war in Vietnam.

The Democratic party paid a price for championing the cause of civil rights in the 1960s. It lost the allegiance of millions of white Southerners who switched to the Republican party at the presidential level. It also seemed to lose its way after a bitter campaign in 1968. Anti-war demonstrators raged outside the Democratic National Convention in the streets of Chicago in 1968. They were furious that Hubert H. Humphrey, the vice president to President Lyndon B. Johnson whom these anti-war protesters held responsible for the war, was being nominated by a convention that was still dominated by old-fashioned ward bosses and elected officials. The anti-war presidential candidates had fallen by the wayside. One, Robert F. Kennedy, the brother of the slain president, had been assassinated in the spring of that year just moments after winning the California presidential primary. The war in Vietnam and the Democratic party bosses decision to ignore the anti-war sentiment left a legacy of bitterness and brought about significant changes in the way both major political parties, particularly the Democrats, selected their standard bearers. Critics of the Democratic party said these changes made the party captive of its liberal elite and and caused it to lose touch with the concerns of more moderate voters, the very voters who decide the outcome of presidential elections. The Democrats eventually came to be identified as the party of big wasteful government who, left unchecked, would spend and tax the poor American taxpayer into an early grave.

The Republican Party and Presidential Politics

Meanwhile, the Republican Party came to be viewed as the party of Middle America even though its policies during the 1980s often benefited the very wealthy and big business. Ronald Reagan won a landslide victory in 1980 over Jimmy Carter because Reagan promised to cut taxes, increase military spending, and reduce the size of government. Reagan was a former movie star who had become the governor of California, the largest state in the country. He had once been a Democrat, but his views shifted as he became wealthier and resented the large chunk the federal government took out of his earnings in the form of taxes. He became a deeply conservative man who was profoundly suspicious of government and wary of communist aggression overseas. His election precipitated "the Reagan Revolution," a reversal of a 40-year trend towards centralization of power and influence in government. Reagan delivered on many of his campaign promises by reducing taxes on the wealthiest Americans and by pouring billions of dollars into the Defense Department. He did not succeed in reducing the size of government because of the increase in military spending, but his pro-business policies contributed to the longest period of economic expansion since World War II. The political problem for the Republican party was that the prosperity was not evenly divided among the populace. More millionaires and billionaires were created during Reagan's years in office than at any other time in American history, but his theory that prosperity would "trickle down" to average people did not seem to work. By the end of the term of his Republican successor, George Bush, hundreds of thousands of Americans had lost their jobs and faced dim prospects for the future.

Republican party success at the presidential level had rested on the pillars of low taxation and anti-communism. By 1992, both pillars had turned into spaghetti. During the 1988 campaign, President Bush made his "read my lips" promise to never raise taxes. As the vice president to Ronald Reagan for eight years, Bush had no difficulty in winning the Republican party presidential nomination in 1988 and casting himself as the rightful heir to Reagan who remained popular but was prohibited by law from running for a third term. After President Franklin D. Roosevelt died during his fourth term, the Constitution was changed or amended to limit presidents to two four-year terms. When he accepted the Republican party presidential nomination at the 1988 Republican National Convention in New Orleans, George Bush asked the public to "read my lips . . . no new taxes." He broke that promise in 1990, and his words came back to haunt him in the 1992 campaign.

The End of the Cold War

The anti-communism pillar was also gone because during Bush's term, the Soviet Union dissolved and the communist satellite nations in Eastern Europe had broken away and become independent states again.

After World War II ended, a different type of war called the Cold War began. The two major combatants in this Cold War were the U.S.S.R. and the U.S.A., the communists versus the capitalists. While the U.S.S.R. and the U.S.A. never fought one another directly, they battled for decades through third parties in small skirmishes that sometimes grew to serious battles such as the war in Vietnam. With the fall of communism beginning in 1989, the Cold War ended and with it the advantage enjoyed by the more militaristic Republican party. The decline of a foreign threat shifted the focus of voters to domestic concerns, a traditional advantage for the Democratic party.

An Opening for the Democrats

Clinton and other like-minded Democrats spotted the glimmer of political opportunity in these changes. Clinton was not the first Democrat to get in the race. The first was Paul E. Tsongas, a former one-term senator from Massachusetts who had chosen not to seek reelection to the Senate in 1984 when he discovered he had cancer of the lymph nodes. Tsongas underwent an experimental bone marrow transplant that appeared to cure him of cancer. He said he felt that he had to run for president because he beat the illness. He called it "the obligation of my survival." For most of 1991, he was the only candidate challenging President Bush. Tsongas ran as a truth teller, the first of several candidates who spoke of the harsh realities of the economy and the need to cut back on federal spending programs called "entitlements," which often benefited the middle class and increased taxes. He cautioned voters, "I'm no Santa Claus." Although none of the truth tellers won, each left a distinct imprint on the race by changing public awareness or pushing the candidates who were successful to change their positions on certain issues.

By the fall of 1991, other Democrats were moving into position to run for president, although none of them were considered big names. Some thought this campaign would be a dry run, a practice campaign, for 1996 when Bush could not run for reelection because of the two-term limit on presidents. In addition to Clinton and Tsongas, the other candidates were Senator Tom Harkin of Iowa, an old-fashioned liberal; Senator Bob Kerrey of Nebraska, a baby boomer like Clinton and a Vietnam veteran who had lost part of a leg in combat; Governor Douglas Wilder of Virginia, the first black governor in the United States; and former Governor Jerry Brown of California, an iconoclastic politician who was making his third run for president. Wilder would withdraw from the race before the first contest.

Buchanan's Challenge and Bush's Response

Bush's challengers weren't confined to ambitious Democrats. In December, Bush suddenly faced an unexpected challenge within his own political party from Patrick J. Buchanan, a conservative columnist and television talk show commentator. Although George Bush claimed to be Ronald Reagan's natural conservative heir, the conservatives known as the "New Right" had always been suspicious of Bush and never accepted him as one of them. His father was a Republican senator from Connecticut, Prescott Bush, and Bush came from a wing of the Republican party that had a progressive, more liberal tradition. George Bush had been a strong supporter of Planned Parenthood, an organization that operated many abortion clinics, but he switched his position and became an opponent of legal abortion when Reagan chose him to be his running mate in 1980. In politics, this switch is known as a political conversion, and many conservatives questioned Bush's sincerity and conviction.

At first, Buchanan had no intention of running for president. He made a lot of money as a private citizen by writing and appearing on television, publishing a newsletter, and delivering speeches. He had never held public office, although he had worked in the White House as a speech writer and policy adviser. But the pugnacious Buchanan was a devout follower of Ronald Reagan, and he felt that Bush had betrayed the Reagan Revolution. During the Thanksgiving Day holiday weekend in 1991, he spoke to his younger sister Angela, who was known by her nickname Bay, by telephone. Bay Buchanan is an active Republican in her home state of California. She urged her brother to run for president and offered to be his campaign manager. Weeks later in December, Buchanan entered the race, just 10 weeks before the New Hampshire primary, the first primary election contest of the nominating season.

While Buchanan faced the longest of odds, he fit snugly into a pattern of intraparty challengers who did not win but did change the course of the campaign and left behind the cuts of a thousand knives on their opponents. Modern political history showed that an internal challenge to a powerful incumbent president is far from an exercise in futility. Presidents Harry S. Truman, Lyndon B. Johnson, Gerald R. Ford, and Jimmy Carter confronted challengers within their own political parties. In all four cases, the opposing party won in November; this proved to be the case in 1992 as well. Buchanan's campaign effectively fizzled by mid-March, although he stayed the course and remained in the race for the entire nominating season. But as a credible conservative critic, Buchanan had impact when he charged that the emperor wore no clothes.

Buchanan's challenge kept Bush from consolidating the Republican party base and led to serious political errors by the Bush organization, particularly at the Republican National Convention in Houston, later in the year.

The world changed dramatically during George Bush's term in office, but George Bush did not change. Bush would be the last Cold War president whose outlook and philosophy was molded by the chilly winds of anti-communist sentiment. When Bush was born in 1924, Prohibition, the Constitutional amendment that forbade the sale of alcoholic beverages, was still in effect. Calvin Coolidge was reelected president that year and Gloria Swanson, a goddess of the silent screen, was still a headlining movie star. Bush had been one of the nation's youngest fighter pilots in World War II. He made a fortune in the oil fields of Texas after the war before entering public service. By 1992, he was a cold warrior wandering around a little bit lost in the new world order. In a famous televised exchange in 1988, Ted Koppel, the ABC newsman, had told Governor Michael S. Dukakis, the Democrats' snakebitten nominee, that he just didn't get it. In 1992, the same was often said of George Bush when he insisted the economy was in great shape when most Americans were having a more difficult time making ends meet.

THE AFTEREFFECTS OF THE 1988 CAMPAIGN

By 1992, many Americans were complaining that presidential campaigns were too long, too expensive, too negative, and too trite. The criticism was valid. The 1988 presidential campaign in which Bush beat Dukakis, the governor of Massachusetts, was so long, expensive, negative, and trite that it triggered a reaction by politicians, the press, and the public in 1992. There was a determination to make the campaign more issue oriented and more relevant to real people. Although this campaign veered into silliness from time to time, it was more meaningful than the contest of four years earlier.

Gary Hart and the Character Issue

The 1988 campaign was the first presidential campaign in which the issue of presidential character dominated much of the discourse. The discussion was prompted by the candidacy of Senator Gary Hart of Colorado, a rangy cowboy-like youthful politician who had started in national politics as the campaign manager for George S. McGovern in the 1972 presidential campaign. The McGovern campaign was the seminal political experience for a generation of Democratic campaign operatives. With the war in Vietnam still raging by the time of Nixon's reelection in 1972, anti-war sentiment solidified behind McGovern, a liberal senator from South Dakota. For many young opponents of the war, the McGovern campaign offered an opportunity to change the political system from within. A young man from Arkansas, Bill Clinton, was McGovern's state coordinator in Texas. Like many other activists from that campaign, Clinton took to heart McGovern's request that they stay involved in the political process and not give up.

Gary Hart was another. He offered himself as the candidate of new ideas when he first ran for president in 1984. His appeal threatened to derail the front-running candidacy of Walter F. Mondale who had been Carter's vice president. Hart won the New Hampshire primary, the first contest, in a landslide and beat Mondale consistently in subsequent primary and caucus fights until the Mondale campaign, which was better financed and enjoyed the support of traditional Democratic party constituencies such as organized labor, was able to right itself. Hart ran out of money and steam in 1984. Mondale won the Democratic party presidential nomination but lost the general election in a landslide to the popular Reagan. By 1988, Hart was ready to try again.

His candidacy, however, had barely gotten off the ground before he sustained the equivalent of a SCUD missile attack. Hart had been married for more than 20 years but was dogged by rumors that he had been unfaithful to his wife Lee. He confronted these rumors by challenging the press to follow him in 1988. One newspaper, the *Miami Herald*, did and apparently caught him in a relationship with a young Florida woman named Donna Rice. The controversy raised serious questions about Hart's suitability to be president. Critics said that it was not so much that he violated his marriage vows but that he behaved in a rash and hypocritical manner. Hart withdrew from the presidential race within weeks of the initial *Miami Herald* disclosures.

Dukakis and Bush

Because Hart was viewed as the frontrunner in 1988, his withdrawal from the race opened the way for Dukakis. Although Dukakis was not well-known nationally except among party activists, he was the candidate with the deepest pockets, that is, the ability to raise a lot of campaign money, and the best understanding of the nominating process. Dukakis was a marathoner who stoically and stolidly plowed his way to the Democratic nomination in 1988. He outlasted his opponents and won because he had the money, fortitude, and personal characteristics that his opponents lacked. He won because of who he was rather than what he stood for, and this became the soft underbelly of his candidacy, which was effectively attacked by George Bush.

Bush attacked Dukakis relentlessly as a wild-eyed liberal who was soft on crime and communism, insensitive to the beliefs of average Americans, and recklessly unreliable with taxpayers' money. Dukakis ignored the attacks until it was too late. Because the public did not know Dukakis well, the public image of him became the graphically unattractive picture being painted by his opponent. The campaign became dominated by symbols. Bush

Bill Clinton learned well the lessons from the defeat of the 1988 Democratic presidential candidate, Michael S. Dukakis. The day after he won the presidency, Clinton called Dukakis and credited him with having paved the way to his victory. (Photo by Stan Grossfeld, *Boston Globe*.)

actually campaigned in an American flag factory in New Jersey one day and literally wrapped himself in the red, white, and blue. It was the same day Dukakis was releasing his plan for national health care coverage, but the picture of Bush and the flags was the one that lingered in the public mind.

A convicted murderer who escaped while on furlough from a Massachusetts prison also became a kind of grim poster-boy for the 1988 campaign. William Robert Horton, Jr., who was known by his nickname Willie, failed to return to prison from a weekend furlough, fled from Massachusetts, and was arrested ten months later in Maryland and charged with breaking into the home of a young couple, terrorizing and assaulting them. Two vivid campaign commercials, one featuring a scary photograph of the African-American convict, sent a powerful message that Dukakis was far outside of the American mainstream.

As a result of this campaign, Bush won and Dukakis lost, but Bush sowed the seeds of his eventual defeat in that campaign. He won because he was not Michael Dukakis not because of what he promised to do as president. The political process is ultimately about the business of governing and the business of ideas, and this made Bush vulnerable in 1992. Voters were in a serious frame of mind in 1992. They felt uneasy about the future and uncertain about their economic well-being. Many worried that they would not be able to educate their children or buy homes. They worried that their children would not do as well as they had done. This made them willing to gamble and vote for change in 1992. Change became the watchword of the year.

Chapter 2

Warming Up: Raising Funds and Generating Momentum

JERRY BROWN AS TRUTH TELLER

Jerry Brown, the former governor of California, decided to run for president in 1992 because of money. He was not running to make money but to make a statement about the insidious influence of money in politics. Money is the mother's milk of politics. This saying is one of the most exhausted of political cliches, but like most cliches, it contains a lot of truth. In modern times, it has become even truer because a political campaign is an exercise in communication. The modern way to communicate a campaign message is through television and radio. Purchasing the airtime for television and radio commercials is typically the most expensive part of any campaign for public office. Brown, an iconoclastic Californian politician, became, like Tsongas, another one of the truth tellers of 1992. While he did not win the election, his candidacy had an impact on the process and influenced the behavior and positions of the man who did win, Bill Clinton.

When Brown formally entered the 1992 Democratic presidential race, he did it far from his home state of California. He chose instead to make his declaration of candidacy standing in front of Independence Hall in Philadelphia, a building fraught with significance in American history. This building was the birthplace of democracy in America where the Constitutional Convention had written the U.S. Constitution, the document that established the U.S. government and political system. More than 200 years later, Brown called for a second American revolution, an uprising of people to reclaim their democracy back from the special and vested interests. His campaign literature headlined the opening words of the U.S. Constitution, "We the people."

This position was a remarkable turn of events for Brown because when he was governor for eight years, he raised millions of dollars to finance his political campaigns. When he was chairman of the Democratic party in his home state, he raised millions more to finance state and local Democratic campaigns. He said that the experience of always going hat in hand to the wealthy had opened his eyes. It was wrong, he said, because the wealthy could purchase access to influence and access to power that was beyond the reach of the average person with their money and influence.

THE ROLE OF MONEY AND PACS IN ELECTIONS

By 1992, nearly every member of Congress who sought reelection won, in large part because incumbents were better financed than challengers. During the 1991 and 1992 election cycle, about half of the $190 million raised by House members for their campaigns came from political action committees. A political action committee, called a PAC for short, is a way for like-minded individuals from private industry or some other interest to put their money together and channel it to politicians who support their point of view. PACs represent a wide range of interests from labor union members to insurance company executives. By 1992, political action committees were giving ten times more money to incumbents than to challengers. The Speaker of the U.S. House, Thomas Foley of Washington, received 72 percent of his contributions from PACs during the '92 campaign.

While PACs were seen as part of the problem by the 1990s, political action committees were actually designed to minimize the role of the wealthy special interest in politics. PACs were part of the sweeping campaign finance reform adopted in 1974, the same year the Watergate scandal forced Richard M. Nixon to resign the presidency. Until the adoption of the campaign finance law in 1974, politicians could accept unlimited amounts of money from wealthy contributors and business interests, and they often did. These rich givers expected to have an open door and a ready ear from the politicians after the election in return for their contributions. Although wealthy individuals were as entitled to representation as poor people, critics warned that the special, narrow interest of a big shot contributor might prevail over the public interest that benefited most of the people.

PACs, however, did not solve the problem. Campaign reform slapped a $5,000 lid on PAC contributions for each election. The reformers did not anticipate that the reform would lead to a rabbit-like proliferation of powerful PACs. For members of Congress who needed more and more money to run for reelection, the interest groups became a ready source of donations. These groups invariably expected something in return. Medical doctors, for example, used the American Medical Association PAC to give money to members of Congress who opposed national health insurance just as the United Auto Workers' PAC gave money to politicians who backed laws beneficial to their members such as strike breaker legislation.

Brown's Protest Against PACs

Brown came from the most conventional of political backgrounds, but he was a most unconventional politician. His father, Edmund G. Brown, Sr., who was known as Pat, had been a popular governor of California. His sister, Kathleen, was the state treasurer in California. Jerry Brown had served two terms as governor of California and run for president twice, in 1976 and in 1980. He was a politician who marched to his own private drummer. When he became governor, he canceled the governor's private jet, sold the governor's bullet proof limousine, and declined to live in the opulent governor's mansion and instead slept on a mattress on the floor of an inexpensive apartment he rented near the State House in Sacramento. When Brown left public life, he studied Zen Buddhism in Japan and worked with the destitute and sick at a clinic in India. He had studied for the priesthood as a young man, and though he decided not to become a Jesuit priest, he never married, lived a simple life, and always retained a spiritual aura for someone involved in the gritty business of politics, despite his gold Rolex wristwatch and a penchant for well-tailored, double-breasted suits.

The campaign finance rules for federal elections limited individual contributions to $1,000 and PAC contributions to $5,000. Jerry Brown went one better than the law and limited all contributions to his campaign to $100. He also set up a toll-free 800 telephone number—1-800-426-1112—which he recited like a Hindu mantra. The toll-free number made it easy for contributors to call and pledge $100 and become involved in his crusade. Brown's message hit a responsive chord with voters because voters were frustrated with the gridlock in the federal government between a Republican president and Democratic Congress that could not seem to agree on anything. Voters were also angry because Congress seemed to have become more responsive to the special interests than the public interests.

As the incumbent president, George Bush, shown here with wife Barbara and Vice President Dan Quayle and his wife Marilyn, was able to raise more money than his Republican primary opponents. (Photo courtesy of the Bush Presidential Materials Project of the National Archives.)

The House Banking Scandal

Congress as an institution was also under fire because many members had allegedly bounced checks at the House bank. The House bank was not really a bank. It was a direct deposit system for congressional paychecks, and the bounced checks were actually advances on pay. But voters sensed that their representatives in Washington had gotten out of touch with the public's concerns and, voters were also primed to believe that the officials in Washington were enjoying perquisites, or favors, and special treatment. So the so-called House bank scandal acquired symbolic significance far beyond the seriousness of the alleged infractions, and it made the public all the more receptive to Brown's efforts.

Jerry Brown marched into this campaign with the fervor of a convert. At first, he drew few followers. The political press found it difficult to take him seriously. From the national press perspective, Brown was a two-time presidential loser who was making a third run without the support staff, platform, or financial resources of a traditional campaign. He didn't even look presidential as he campaigned in cold New England in a white turtleneck jersey that made him look like the priest he had once considered becoming. He openly acknowledged that this was a crusade, a movement, not a conventional campaign. "This is a campaign that will not behave. This campaign will not sit down when it is told to sit down," he said one day while campaigning in New Hampshire. At candidate debates, Brown recited his 800 number even when told that it was inappropriate. At one debate, he began reading a newspaper. He was criticized for behaving in a rude manner, but he later explained that he was reading a copy of the *Philadelphia Inquirer* newspaper series on what was wrong with America. The installment he was reading dealt with the corruption inherent in political finance. He was doing research. It was all very strange, but people were listening.

BUILDING UP THE WAR CHEST

Running for president is an expensive proposition. It is the equivalent of throwing together a multimillion dollar company virtually overnight. A candidate needs a plan, a purpose, and lots of money or at least enough money to be seen as credible. Credibility is one of the many "touchy feely" things about politics and political campaigns that is difficult for casual observers to understand but is absolutely critical to the success or failure of the candidate. If a candidate is seen as credible, then the candidate is taken more seriously. Credibility in this case means the capability of going all the way and winning the election.

Clinton's Fundraising

The Boston-area businessman who raised millions for Michael Dukakis' presidential campaign in 1988, Robert Farmer, often said that money was the first primary contest. In 1988, Dukakis won that primary hands down by raising far more money than his opponents, well over $10 million by the end of 1987. In 1992, the Democrats who had access to the big contributors, potential candidates like

Bill Clinton, shown here the day after winning the election, was able to raise more money than his Democratic opponents. (Photo by Joanne Rathe, *Boston Globe*.)

Governor Mario Cuomo of New York, who as governor of a large and prosperous state knew many people who would help finance his campaign, chose not to run. The group of Democrats who did run were relative paupers with limited access to big bucks. Clinton, however, wooed Farmer to his side in 1991. Just signing up the man who was known as a Democratic Midas capable of spinning much gold for his favored candidate gave the governor of Arkansas an instant shot of credibility. The political professionals and press people who do the early handicapping in presidential campaigns could say to themselves, "Well, if Farmer is with him, he must have a chance."

Farmer also produced for Clinton. Farmer and Rahm Emmanual, the slight former ballet dancer who was the finance director for the campaign, scheduled 26 fundraisers in 20 days in December 1991 and resisted intense pressure from the New Hampshire campaign staff for more of Clinton's time. The Clinton schedulers needed to balance the long-range financial needs of the campaign against the amount of time needed to make a credible showing in New Hampshire. At this point, Clinton did not need to come in first in New Hampshire; he just needed to make a good showing. (It was expected that Tsongas had to win because he came from Massachusetts, a neighboring state.) As a result of all the fundraisers, Clinton ended the year with $3.3 million in the till. He had more money in the bank than any other Democratic candidate, money that became critically important when his campaign hit rocky roads during the New Hampshire primary campaign and later. His financial cushion allowed him to spend an extra $1 million in New Hampshire when hit by the double whammy of charges of infidelity and draft dodging, an extra $600,000 in Georgia, an extra $700,000 in New York and Wisconsin to deal with the unexpected Jerry Brown threat, and an extra $1.2 million in California, the final primary that represented one-fifth of the electoral college votes needed in November to be elected president.

Buchanan's Direct Mail Solicitation

It was easy for President Bush to raise campaign money because he was an incumbent president of the party that had been in power for a long time. His opponent, Pat Buchanan, might have had a lot of difficulty raising money from traditional Republican party sources who would be reluctant to help someone challenging the sitting president of their own party. So he ignored those traditional Republican givers, and he chose instead to raise money from conservatives through the mail in small amounts. This method is called direct mail solicitation, and it is the way in which the New Right conservative political movement has traditionally financed itself. The cause or, in Buchanan's case, the candidate, sends a letter requesting funds to people who have been previously identified as sympathetic to the conservative point of view because they signed a petition or gave money to another conservative cause. Buchanan wrote his own solicitation letters that were so effective that he was able to qualify for federal matching funds in record time. A candidate for president can match each small campaign contribution with money from a special federal fund by raising $5,000 in 20 different states in amounts of $250 or less. The program was designed to provide a level playing field for politicians who were not personally wealthy. Bush, by contrast, was rolling in the maximum $1,000 contributions from better-heeled givers.

This discrepancy, however, also revealed a critical difference in their appeal. More people were giving to Buchanan than giving to Bush, which indicated a vulnerability in the president. In elections, it is the number of votes that count on election day, and a wealthy contributor only gets one vote just the same as the poorest person who goes to the polls that day. The nature of the contributors also showed another crucial difference between Buchanan and Bush. The people sending money to Buchanan felt more strongly about his candidacy than those giving to Bush. Many of the Bush givers did so out of a sense of duty or because they felt they were expected to support the president. By contrast, Buchanan's givers and supporters were true believers. The Buchanan campaign had more intensity than the president's campaign. In politics, the level of intensity and commitment can make a huge difference.

The Other Democratic Candidates

Meanwhile, the other Democratic candidates who stayed in the race, Paul Tsongas, Tom Harkin, and Bob Kerrey, were having more difficulty raising and saving money for their campaigns. They had to convince people to believe in them and believe that they could win. To be seen as credible, candidates sometimes are forced to spend money as fast as they raise it to conduct public opinion polls, hire staff, open campaign headquarters, travel, print brochures and campaign signs, and do all the other things that give the appearance of a serious political campaign. But money tells only part of the story.

THE PRESEASON CAMPAIGN

A presidential campaign is divided into four distinct parts: *the preseason*, the long months before a single voter casts a ballot when candidates jockey for position in a shadowy world of professional pundits where perception is often more important than reality; *the nominating season,* the period when the candidates compete for the major party nominations in primary and caucus contests; *the nominating conventions*, the summer olympics in politics when the two major parties with great spectacle officially nominate the candidate and prepare for the fall; and *the general election*, the main event when the major candidates square off and campaign for the presidency. While fundraising is one of the most important early barometers used to measure political credibility, it is not the only one.

Polls

For a candidate, the preseason is a time to become a serious candidate by conducting extensive public opinion polling, recruiting a staff, engaging in mock battles such as straw polls among party activists, and developing and sharpening a campaign message. Long before real people actually go to the local caucus in Iowa or go to the polls in New Hampshire on primary day, the politicians who seek the presidency conduct public opinion polls. They use these polls to take the temperature of the electorate and measure the mood of voters. Candidates poll to measure their own potential appeal and strength and to determine the best way to present their message to voters.

Presidential candidates conduct two types of polls, general public opinion polls and focus group polls. Today most public opinion polls are conducted over the telephone by professional pollsters who write questionnaires and hire and train dozens of interviewers who ask the questions. When the interviewer calls a person whose telephone number is chosen at random by a computer, the interviewer asks the same questions of each person. Polls that are limited to registered voters begin by asking each respondent if he or she is a registered voter. If the person is not registered, the interviewer thanks the person and hangs up and tries another number. Drawing a sample is the most difficult part of conducting a poll. To accurately reflect the population at large, the poll hinges upon interviewing the right number of people from different races, backgrounds, and income levels; the right number of men and women; and the right number of liberals, conservatives, and moderates. Polling combines a scientific understanding of statistics with the art of understanding politics. Good pollsters draw on both skills to survey public opinion.

Each poll surveys a sample of people in a given state or across the country and elicits from those answers a statistically valid snapshot of public opinion. Snapshot is the key phrase. A professional poll can usually provide an accurate reading of public opinion at the time in which the poll was conducted, but public opinion can change rapidly depending upon the events of the moment. A poll that is valid and accurate on Monday can be totally wrong on Friday if a major event takes place on Wednesday. Many professional politicians were blinded by the public opinion polls conducted after the Persian Gulf War that showed about 90 per-

In 1992, voters told pollsters that the country was heading in the wrong direction. Cartoonist Dan Wasserman portrayed them as sending out a distress signal. (Cartoon by Dan Wasserman, Boston Globe, distributed by LA Times Syndicate.)

cent of the American public had a favorable opinion of President Bush. Months later, when concerns about the economy grew and the afterglow from the successful war dimmed, voter opinion of Bush changed.

To conduct a valid public opinion poll, a pollster must interview at least 300 people. Most national polls entail interviews with more than 1,000 people. The larger the sample or number of people interviewed, the more accurate the poll; however, polls are not perfect. A pollster can ask a question in several different ways that will elicit different types of answers, and so good pollsters attempt to ask questions in a neutral way that will not provoke a biased response. All polls have what is called a margin of error, which means that the poll result is accurate within a certain number of points. The larger the sample, the smaller the margin of error. So in a poll of 1,000 people in which voters are asked to choose between two candidates, the poll results will be accurate within a small, statistical margin of error—plus or minus three percentage points. If candidate A receives 40 points and candidate B receives 60 points, candidate A's actual support can range from 37 to 43 points while candidate B's support may be from 57 to 63 percentage points.

Focus group polls are not really polls at all but are small intimate sessions with a dozen or so voters who spend several hours with a trained leader discussing in depth their views on issues and candidates. Candidates increasingly use these types of sessions to acquire more insight into voter reaction to television and radio advertisements and to probe negative opinions that are uncovered in a more superficial way in a regular public opinion poll.

The horse race numbers, which are the poll results that show who is ahead and who is trailing, get the most attention, but unless the election is only days away, political professionals consider other numbers in the poll more significant. During a political campaign, the number of voters with a favorable or unfavorable opinion of a politician can be crucial. The firmness of commitment to a candidate and his or her positions is also very important because voters who feel strongly about a candidate and share the same point of view are less likely to abandon that candidate if the campaign gets rough. Consider these numbers. In a poll of 306 Democratic primary voters in New Hampshire on January 20 and

21 in 1992 conducted by Political/ Media Research, Bill Clinton was ahead with 32 percent followed by Paul Tsongas at 27, Bob Kerrey at 11, Tom Harkin at 8, and Jerry Brown at 3. Another 19 percent of these respondents who identified themselves as voters likely to vote in the Democratic primary said that they were undecided. This poll had a margin of error of plus or minus 5.5 percentage points. A political professional reading these results would say that Clinton and Tsongas were in a statistical dead heat because of the margin of error. Clinton had been leading by a wider margin earlier in the month, but this poll was conducted immediately after a woman named Gennifer Flowers claimed she had had a 12-year love affair with him. The poll showed that this controversy was hurting Clinton with voters.

Straw Polls

Even before the serious campaigning began in Iowa and New Hampshire, the candidates engaged in preseason skirmishing that usually had no impact on the voters but affected the candicates standing with the insiders who watched politics closely. During the preseason for the 1984 and 1988 campaigns, candidates had aggressively competed in straw polls among party activists. These competitions drained money and time from the candidates, and so by 1992, the Democratic National Committee Chairman Ronald H. Brown sternly advised Democrats to skip these exercises. The Florida Democratic party ignored his advice and held a straw poll in December 1991 at Disneyworld, a setting that seemed appropriate for a political exercise that had more to do with the fantasy than with the reality of voting in the Florida primary months later in March or in the general election 11 months later in November.

At the time, John Sasso, who had been Dukakis' campaign manager in 1988, predicted, "A month after this straw poll, the whole event will be totally forgotten . . . It won't tell you anything about the candidates' potential appeal." Sasso's prediction was correct because the first televised candidate debate on NBC totally eclipsed the straw poll in the news. Although the straw poll of Democratic party activists at the Magic Kingdom from December 13 to 15, 1991, was totally forgotten within hours, it did turn out to be instructive because it provided an early glimpse of the political issues that Democrats faced as they began the process of taking back the White House.

Although Florida is located in the South, it is not regarded as part of the Old Confederacy like Alabama and Georgia and other Southern states. Florida, like Texas, is a large and complex state with a distinct political identity. Although both Florida and Texas share some characteristics with more traditional Southern states, political analysts usually examine them separately. For the purposes of the Florida straw poll, however, Florida was being viewed as a Southern state and an early preseason testing ground for Bill Clinton and his Democratic competitors to try out their campaign messages and appeal with active Democrats.

The straw poll cranks up the "expectation game" in national politics. In this game, political professionals attempt to guess how well a candidate will do depending upon prior performance, history, and any number of factors. This game of expectations can be deadly because in the months before real people get involved in the process, the candidates' ability to raise money and recruit supporters can be affected by whether they fall short, meet, or exceed expectations for their performance as determined by a group of political insiders. Although it may not seem fair that a group of self-appointed pundits in the press and in the political community handicap candidates long before real people get involved, this situation is a reality of politics that dates back to the fabled smoke-filled, back rooms when party bosses decided who would run for public office. Party activists and political consultants have replaced the handful of big city mayors and county commissioners who used to handpick the candidates who would stand for election. Straw polls, for all their shortcomings, set up early tests of strength.

For the straw poll, Clinton needed to do very well if not win the competition because he was the governor of a Southern border state. As expectation-game reasoning went, if Clinton could not do well in a Florida straw poll, how could he expect to win the support of real Southern voters on election day. Tom Harkin was from the Midwestern state of Iowa, but he chose to make a strong effort in the straw poll because he was counting on traditional Democratic party constituency groups, particularly liberals and labor unions, to support his candidacy. He thought that if he did very well, he would be taken more seriously as a national candidate. Straw polls of party activists are conducted in a small universe, and organized groups such as labor union members can exert more influence in this type of political exercise than they do in actual, real-life voting. Doug Wilder and Jerry Brown decided to skip the straw poll, and so they were not expected to do well. Paul Tsongas and Bob Kerrey decided to attend but not make a strong effort to minimize expectations for their performances.

As a result of all this positioning, the stakes were highest for Clinton and Harkin. Even at this early point in the presidential campaign, Clinton was being seen as a potential frontrunner. He could not afford to be embarrassed. Harkin needed to prove himself a serious national contender. So both campaigns went to work to recruit support. At the Buena Vista Palace in Orlando, Florida, the Harkin and Clinton campaigns set up television sets to show campaign videos that were designed to convince these Democrats who was the best candidate for the presidency. Because so many voters had VCRs, many campaigns used videocassettes to communicate with voters in 1992.

This weekend in Florida also exposed one of the fundamental struggles within the Democratic party in 1992: the fight between traditional Democratic liberals, represented by Harkin, and younger Democrats who claimed to be different and new and argued that the party needed to change to win the White House. Clinton proved to be the strongest candidate from this "new Democrat" group.

The straw poll exercise was a warm-up for the candidates, a chance to try out their messages and styles on Democratic activists. Harkin wore a plaid shirt in his video to show he was just a regular guy and to convince voters that he was a champion for the average workers. The video told about his life including his service in the U.S. Navy. The senator was shown communicating with his brother Frank, who is deaf, with sign language. With inspirational music rising in the background, Harkin made an emotional appeal for support. "Together," he said, "we'll build that new America."

Harkin, like other Democratic presidential candidates, realized that people were worried about the economy. His answer was to use federal government money to build public works projects, the same answer used after the Great Depression in the 1930s to get people back to work. This position was a traditional Democratic party response to bad economic times. When he spoke to all of the delegates, he appeared feisty and used strong language to convince these activists that he was willing to battle with the Republicans.

"It's time to fight," he told them."I'm going to make George Herbert Walker Bush apologize for what he has done to America . . . It's time for us to take our traditional Democratic values to the American people."

All of the Democratic candidates were critical of President Bush because trashing the Republicans is a surefire way to stir up partisan Democrats. "We know the Cold War is over," said Senator Kerrey who entered the hall to the strains of Bruce Springsteen hit "Born to Run." "The era of the cold warriors has ended as well . . . Our Cold War president has got cold feet." Kerrey would base his presidential campaign on his proposal to scrap the existing system for financing health care with a new system that would extend coverage to all Americans.

"The man who brought us voodoo economics has become the witch doctor of American health care," he said. "For 12 years, we've been waiting in Dr. Bush's waiting room . . . . On the issue of health care, Dr. Bush is guilty of malpractice and in 1992 it is time for America to revoke his license to practice." After being shot in Vietnam, Kerrey spent years recovering from his injuries in Veterans Administration hospitals. He said that the U.S. government had saved his life, and he felt, much like Tsongas who had survived cancer, that he had an obligation to help others.

The low-key Paul Tsongas was the only candidate who did not attempt to make a dramatic entrance from the

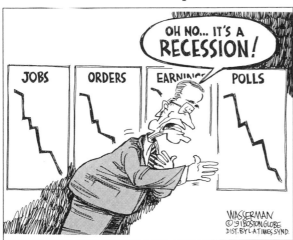

President Bush insisted that the economy was in good shape but changed his tune when his popularity dropped. (Cartoon by Dan Wasserman, *Boston Globe*, distributed by LA Times Syndicate.)

rear of the hall. He walked to the podium to some sort of nameless New Age music, which seemed to fit with his quirky political personna. Tsongas spoke about the decline of America as an economic force. "The Reagan-Bush record is very clear: We are selling off our country and we are leaving our children to pay it off," he said in his earnest way. "America is hurting. The Cold War is over and Japan won, Germany won, Taiwan won, and Switzerland won." He accused the Republicans of engaging in "Twinkie economics; it tastes good but has no nutritional value."

Tsongas' words elicited much nodding from the Democrats. "The American people don't trust us with the economy," he said. "That is our fault. That is why we lose. Some Democrats say losing is good for your character. I've got enough character." His argument for a policy of economic nationalism that would restore the nation's manufacturing jobs by providing incentives to business made sense to many of these activists, although most said they could not imagine how this quiet, self-deprecating man could ever win a presidential election.

Clinton's Straw Poll Truimph

If Tsongas lost the charisma contest, then Clinton won it. Clinton entered the darkened hall to the theme from "Chariots of Fire." A spotlight sought him out and lit his way as he worked the crowd and made his way to the stage. His wife Hillary introduced him.

"George Bush is presiding over the destruction of the middle class," charged Clinton. "He has turned the office of president into a spectator sport." He accused Bush of being more concerned about foreign policy than problems in the United States, a charge that would become a major issue during the campaign. "We have a president who can come out with a plan for the economic troubles of the Soviet Union in five days but cannot decide in five months what to do for America," he said. "We don't need to elect the last president of the twentieth century. We need to elect the first president of the twenty-first century." Clinton put himself forward as not only a member of a different generation but as someone with a different approach to the job of president. "I propose a new way of doing government," he said. His approach required people to take more responsibility for themselves and not look to the government first. He said that he would not propose a program for every problem. In his video, he told the Democrats, "This is not just a campaign, this is a crusade for the soul of America."

The Clinton campaign understood that successful politics contains both substance and glitz. They buried the opposition in the straw poll competition by making the Florida activists feel courted, important, and involved. The Clinton campaign had mailed 1,000 of the 16-minute videos to state Democratic Convention delegates the week before and hand delivered another 1,000 videos. Although Harkin had an advantage at first because he enjoyed strong support from labor unions, which do a good job of organizing their members behind a single candidate, Clinton began to pick up support because the party activists were impressed by the personal touch. While Harkin distributed free drink tickets at the door of a reception for delegates, Clinton left personalized messages on the hotel voice mail system for delegates registered at the hotel.

The Clinton campaign out-organized the others. Operatives worked the convention floor with walkie-talkies. Each delegate found a fortune cookie at their dinner seat that contained a message:

A Secret Service agent grips President George Bush's belt to make sure he is not pulled into the crowd. (Photo courtesy of the Bush Presidential Materials Project of the National Arhives.)

Bill Clinton is in your future. The Clinton campaign also provided t-shirts printed up just for this weekend that boasted, "I made history." Democrats were tired of losing presidential campaigns and desperate to win in 1992, and so a lot of liberal Democrats who might have been put off by Clinton's challenges to liberal orthodxy were more willing to consider a candidate like him. "If you want to win again," he said at the end of his speech, "I'm your man."

It worked. Clinton captured more than half of the 1,771 votes cast, 54 percent, followed by Harkin at 31 percent, Kerrey at 10 percent. Tsongas only got 32 votes, less than 2 percent, only eight more votes than Doug Wilder who did not even attend. Jerry Brown barely registered with only four votes. Mario Cuomo, who was not even a candidate, received more than 20 write-in votes from delegates. "I want to win in 1992," said one Dade County realtor of Clinton. "He looks like a winner."

By the time the results were counted and announced, all of the candidates had left Florida to fly to Washington to appear on the first joint televised appearance of the campaign, a debate hosted by NBC's Tom Brokaw. Clinton left behind a statement: "It's gratifying that people from diverse backgrounds all across Florida have embraced my message of restoring the middle class, re-inventing government, and getting the economy moving again. What this convention has shown is a message that brings people together instead of driving them apart can win. This is just the first step. Now we will build on this victory to win Florida in March—and in November."

THE IMPORTANCE OF CAMPAIGN STAFF

The straw poll also revealed a level of technical expertise in the Clinton campaign that would become important at critical junctures in the campaign. Campaign tactics and staff are not enough in and of themselves to win an election—a candidate also needs a compelling message that resonates with voters—but in the competitive world of presidential politics, experience and expertise count and can make a crucial difference when the going gets rough. Behind every candidate for public office stands a massive human machine of campaign workers. The best and most experienced workers make up a type of political subculture with its own customs, traditions, and practices. The elite from this subculture plot the strategy and execute the plans for the greatest democratic exercise in the world. They are the hired guns of politics, the wranglers who ride the campaign range. They have not only become a permanent part of the campaign environment, but they have also become an essential element as political campaigns have grown more complex and the challenge of communicating a message to millions of people more daunting. While Ross Perot claimed he was not a typical politician and disdained the hired guns, he ended up hiring two of the best-known campaign operatives in the country to run the first phase of his campaign. For his second campaign in October, he chose not to use professional strategists, but he went to professionals to produce the campaign commercials that were regarded as among the most effective of the year.

For all their technical expertise at building crowds and running rallies, writing speeches, producing television commercials, or administering complex and chaotic campaigns, most political pros are fundamentally political junkies who believe that they can be agents of change within the political system. They are surprisingly ideological. The Democrats' staff tends to be as liberal as the Republicans' staff is conservative. Rarely will operatives work for a candidate whom they cannot personally support.

Michael Whouley

Clinton could point to a campaign consultant from Boston for his success in Orlando, a political professional named Michael Whouley. At the time of the straw poll, Whouley was 32 years old, an intense young man who never seemed to be still. Even while sitting, his knee jiggled, his fingers tapped out a relentless beat, and he smoked cigarettes incessantly. Whouley would be only one of the hundreds of people who worked behind the scenes to get Bill Clinton into the White House. While he had unusual talent as a political organizer, he was also a typical Democratic operative because he worked only for Democrats, and despite his tough-guy reputation, he cared about and believed that politics could make life better for average people.

Nearly everyone called him by his last name, "Whouley." He grew up in St. Peter's parish in the Dorchester section of Boston, a neighborhood where little boys did literature drops in political campaigns instead of Little League. He was the oldest of three children of a consulting engineer from South Boston. He graduated from Boston College where he majored in philosophy and political science. Like many people from his neighborhood, politics was always part of his life. He could remember talking about the 1968 presidential campaign when he was only eight years old. When he was 14, he distributed campaign brochures for a neighbor who ran for the state legislature. At the age of 20 he was the youngest ward coordinator in a Boston mayoral campaign in 1979.

For all his old-fashioned training, Whouley was also on the cutting edge of change in political campaigns in 1992. He helped to create a different structure and method of operation for delivering a campaign message to voters. Just as he had videotapes hand delivered door to door to Florida straw poll participants, he did the same thing in New Hampshire with real voters in a unique marriage of shoe leather and high technology. He would turn the old-fashioned "Get Out The Vote" or GOTV part of the campaign into something called "Get On TV" in the Clinton campaign, where even low level aides did things to get television coverage for the campaign.

CONCLUSION

By January, all of the candidates were staffed and ready to go. The serious business of convincing real voters to support them was about to begin.

The 1992 campaign interrupted a modern trend towards a prolonged warm-up period of the campaign. The serious mind-set of voters who were demanding real answers from presidential hopefuls, the relatively limited resources of the candidates, the reduced news budgets of media organizations suffering from the recession, and the delayed start of active campaigning because of Bush's popularity in 1991, effectively shortened the preseason to a matter of a few months in the late fall. Not only did voters prefer a shorter campaign, but the growing expense of a modern presidential campaign suggested that the 1992 model might be the wave of the future.

Chapter 3

Retailing: The Iowa Caucus and New Hampshire Primary

Every four years, the road to the White House begins in Iowa and New Hampshire, the states where the first caucus and first primary election are held. To win a major party presidential nomination, a candidate must secure more delegate votes than any other candidate at the nominating conventions that are held during the summer. Candidates accrue delegates by winning state caucuses and primary elections. Under the rules of each major party, each state is allocated a certain number of delegate votes. That number is determined by a formula that weighs factors such as the population of the state and the number of people who voted for the party's presidential candidate in the last election. A candidate can run for president as an independent candidate or member of a minor political party without going through this procedure, but that candidate must go through a laborious process of collecting voter signatures to get on the ballot in each state. In 1992, a Texas billionaire named Ross Perot did just that.

But before Perot appeared on the political scene, the Democrats and Republicans who wanted to be president were busy dialing the 515 and 603 area codes in Iowa and New Hampshire to begin the painstaking process of winning over key community leaders and average individuals one vote at a time. In politics, this process of going door to door and introducing oneself to voters and asking for support or standing in a living room on a chilly January night in Keene, New Hampshire, or Dubuque,

Iowa, and making a fervent pitch to a dozen people from the neighborhood is known as retailing. In commerce, merchants buy in bulk from wholesalers and sell the product off one at time to individual retail clients. Politics is much the šame way at the beginning of the nominating season. Later in the season, the candidates go wholesale in larger states by advertising more heavily on television and radio. But in Iowa and New Hampshire, one-on-one contact still matters.

THE ORIGINS OF PRIMARIES

Although some convention delegates were first elected through primaries in 1908, the real power rested with party activists, elected officials, and the local political powerhouses known as bosses— the political pros of the pre-media age. They decided among themselves who to put up as their party's nominee for president. When John F. Kennedy won the presidency in 1960, only a handful of states held primary elections and caucuses in which candidates could truly compete for support. That situation began to change after the Democrats' controversial convention in 1968 when the party insiders picked Hubert H. Humphrey, the vice president to President Lyndon B. Johnson, to be the party nominee and ignored the Democrats who were calling for a change in Johnson's decision to escalate the war in Vietnam. Humphrey's nomination created such discord within the party that there was a call for reform. A reform commission headed by Senator George S. McGovern of South Dakota came up with a plan to make the nominating process more open to real Democratic voters and to take the power to choose nominees away from the bosses.

McGovern learned the new rules of the road so well that he won the party nomination himself in 1972, the very next presidential election. McGovern opposed the war in Vietnam and channeled anti-war sentiment into a powerful force that roared through the primary and caucus season and catapulted him to the nomination. He lost the election to Richard M. Nixon, but the McGovern Commission began a trend towards more participation by regular Democrats. In 1968, there were only 17 presidential primaries. In 1992, there were more than 40. The Republicans had their own set of specific rules, but they, too, followed the trend toward more participation by average voters in picking party nominees.

This trend had many unanticipated side effects. It made the campaign longer as candidates began searching for support earlier and earlier and contributed to the professionalization of the political operatives who became more and more important as the process became more complicated. This trend also contributed to the decline in power of political parties and party leaders because any candidate with a compelling message and the means to deliver that message could make an end run around the party apparatus and capture the nomination. A little-known ex-governor from Georgia, Jimmy Carter, did that in 1976 to win the Democratic nomination over more established and better-known politicians.

The Role of Political Parties in the Primaries

Political parties are supposed to stand for specific positions and points of view. Voters who share that point of view, who believe, for example, as Democrats do, that government should play a significant role in improving the economy by regulating business and setting a minimum wage, will join that party and work for the election of the party candidates. Those who share the Republican philosophy that government should keep its hands out of business and let the market economy work on its own without any interference can join the Republican party and support the Republican candidates for public office.

Years ago, party discipline was far more rigorous than it is today. The political party played a social service role that in modern times has been assumed by government entitlement programs. Earlier in the century, in city neighborhoods filled with immigrants and first generation Americans, an unemployed worker would go to the party boss for a loan, some food, or even a job—often a public works job on the city payroll or for a contractor who held a city contract. In return, the boss expected that person to vote for the party's slate of candidates in the next election.

Today, although some voters still feel strongly about their political affiliation, the ties of loyalty that bind voters to their party have grown weaker because the government now provides benefits to everyone in need regardless of political view. Other social factors, such as improved education, also led to the decline of political parties. Voters can read newspapers and listen to radio and television news and make up their own minds about politics and no longer need to blindly obey a party boss. The movement from the cities to the suburbs after World War II also changed lifestyles; families live more separate and independent lives than those their parents and grandparents lived in the city.

By 1992, millions of American voters considered themselves independent voters who voted for the man or woman they liked rather than the candidate of a particular party. Others were gravitating towards new political parties that were built around single issues or concerns such as the environment or anti-tax sentiment. Because of television and radio, anyone had the potential to run for president and become well known in a short period of time. Instant communication made it possible to become a national celebrity within hours or days. Voters were also increasingly unhappy with the status quo by the end of George Bush's term in office, and that status quo included both Democrats and Republicans.

Even some of the candidates from the traditional parties were ready to break party ties. Jerry Brown was a Democrat, but he declared a pox on the houses of both the Democrats and Republicans in Washington during his campaign. He said that the two parties had merged into one "incumbent party" in Washington that worked for the special interests rather than the people. "Some call themselves liberals, some call themselves conservatives, but they are all bought and paid for by the top one percent," he charged one day while campaigning in Pennsylvania. This sort of rhetoric resonated with a lot of unhappy voters during the campaign.

The Importance of the Iowa Caucus

The Iowa caucus became important in 1976 when an obscure peanut farmer from Georgia, Jimmy Carter, won the allegiance of many party activists by promising he would always tell the truth and would give them a government as good as its people. "Undecided" topped the caucus ticket that year. Carter finished second in the actual balloting, but he was the candidate who got the most votes and his "victory" attracted attention that helped him deliver his message to a wider audience and win the later contests. In these

During the retail phase of the presidential campaign, all of the candidates, including presidents, are expected to press the flesh and talk directly to voters, as George Bush is doing in this picture. (Photo courtesy of the Bush Presidential Materials Project of the National Archives.)

early days of the Iowa caucus, it was not very representative of general voter opinion because only a small number of insiders and activists bothered to attend.

Under the caucus system, the party members who live in a particular community all gather at a neighborhood spot such as the fire station, the town hall, or even someone's living room. They divide into groups depending upon which candidate they support. The biggest group carries the day. There are other rules that require each candidate to get a certain percentage of the vote to actually score, called "reaching threshold." Those who fall short of the minimal number needed to be counted—the political term is viable—end up regrouping behind other candidates. As a result, caucus night can be a very complicated, unpredictable, and exciting time as voters swap sides and cut deals at hundreds of caucus sites across the state. Because participants are obliged to stand up and indicate their preference in public, a lot of people who prefer to keep their politics private will not participate. It also takes time to go to caucus, group, and regroup, and so only the most committed voters are willing to invest the time in this democratic exercise.

Although a record number of participants attended the Iowa caucuses in 1988, they constituted barely 10 percent of the voting age population in the state. This relatively low level of participation is something that troubled a lot of political observers. Although the participants tended to be more committed and better informed than the average person, they were also wielding influence greater than their numbers because so many people chose not to be involved. Say, for example, there was an empty lot in a neighborhood that was being used for dumping trash. Of the fifteen families in the neighborhood, only five attend a meeting to figure out what to do about the dump site. Three of those families decide to file a lawsuit against the owner of the lot while the other two think it would make more sense to report the dumping to city officials and organize a neighborhood clean-up crew to clean it up once and for all. The three who outnumber the two prevail while the other ten families in the neighborhood, who would have liked to see the dump site cleaned up and avoid prolonged litigation, relinquish their right to have a say in this neighborhood problem because they skipped the meeting. This scenario happens in presidential politics, too.

Throughout the nominating season, relatively small numbers of voters end up getting involved in the campaign or voting on primary or caucus day. Because the most active Republicans tend to be the most conservative and the most active Democrats tend to be the most liberal, the party nominees tended to reflect the most conservative elements of the Republican party and the most liberal elements of the Democratic party. While the country was in a conservative political cycle, this nominating system made it impossible for the Democratic candidate to win the presidency. Even Democratic voters abandoned the nominees they considered too liberal and voted for the Republicans. These Democrats came to be known as Reagan-Democrats because so many abandoned Jimmy Carter and Walter Mondale to vote for Ronald Reagan. To bring back conservative Democrats, Bill Clinton cast himself as a "new Democrat" who was neither liberal nor conservative, someone who combined elements of both and was new and different. This strategy helped him win.

Field Organization

When there are fewer participants in a political campaign, it is easier to organize them to support a specific candidacy and to get them to the polls on election day. This process is done through a field organization, but it has dwindled in importance as television and radio ads have become a more effective and efficient means of communicating a campaign message. However in New Hampshire and Iowa, the presence of a field organization can make a difference, particularly in a close race. In a typical field structure, the candidate names a state campaign manager who recruits or hires organizers who are responsible for a given geographic area. The organizers run the campaign in a county or congressional district. They make sure campaign literature is distributed door to door by volunteers or mailed. They sometimes write special brochures tailored to address the specific interests or concerns of local voters. They often speak in the candidate's absence at local schools and civic organization meetings. From small satellite campaign headquarters, they contact voters by telephone, mail, or in person, try to convince the voters to support their candidate, and make sure that their voters get to the polls on election day. Field organizers are the grunt workers of politics; to get people to vote, some will even drive voters to their polling spot or baby-sit their children.

IOWA AND NEW HAMPSHIRE IN 1992

Iowa played a major role in doing what is called "winnowing the field" in 1988. There are typically a number of candidates at the beginning of the process, and they must do well in either Iowa or New Hampshire to stay in the race. If they lose, they have a harder time raising campaign funds and signing up supporters. The winners also build up what is called "momentum." This head of steam injects energy and vitality into the candidacy. Winning tends to be a self-fulfilling prophecy. Winners attract money and supporters, which help them keep winning. Candidates who try hard but fail to win support end up falling by the wayside and are "winnowed out" of the process. Politics is a game where the strong prevail over the weak, although strength and weakness are often a matter of luck and timing, of being at the right place at the right time.

The Iowa Bounce

Iowa had assumed legendary importance in presidential politics not only because the contest came first but also because the results had such a major impact on the campaign. In 1984, Walter F. Mondale, the former vice president, was expected to win the Iowa contests because he came from Minnesota, the state next-door, and he was also the front-runner. He did win, but he didn't get much credit for his victory because the collapse of the candidacy of Senator John Glenn of Ohio was bigger news. Glenn, the first U.S. astronaut to circle the globe in outer space, was expected to give Mondale the most trouble. As a result of Glenn's poor showing, the senator from Colorado, Gary Hart, who was not expected to do very well, finished second. Hart finished a very distant second with 16 percent of the vote to Mondale's 49 percent, but something very strange happened. All of a sudden, Hart was seen as THE alternative candidate to the frontrunning Mondale. Hart got what was called the "Iowa bounce"; the spurt of publicity after the caucuses helped propel him to an astonishing victory barely two weeks later in the New Hampshire primary.

The bounce didn't work for Representative Richard Gephardt of Missouri in 1988 because he was favored to win the caucus and he did. And in 1992, Iowa was almost an afterthought because the senior senator from Iowa, Tom Harkin, was one of the Democratic presidential candidates. Few people expected good Iowa Democrats to stand up on caucus night on February 10 and support someone running against their home state senator. So the other Democrats left Iowa to Harkin and went to New Hampshire instead. Although Harkin won the caucus easily, his victory was almost meaningless because no one else played. It was as if all the other players on the opposing basketball team left the court and allowed him to shoot baskets all by himself. He got the most baskets, but no one could consider him the winner of a game. On the Republican side, Patrick J. Buchanan decided to skip Iowa and challenge President Bush in New Hampshire.

The Gateway to the White House

So in 1992, New Hampshire resumed its traditional role as the gateway to the White House, the first critical testing ground of the presidential campaign. Because it is an election, it is considered a more legitimate test for a candidate than a caucus and a more reliable measure of the candidate's appeal to voters. New Hampshire is not representative of the rest of the United States. It is small, mostly white, Republican, and conservative. But since 1952, it has been the scene of the opening act in presidential politics. The New Hampshire primary results have broken many political hearts. Twice the New Hampshire electorate helped convince incumbent presidents not to seek reelection: Harry Truman in 1952 and Lyndon B. Johnson in 1968. In 1992, the New Hampshire Republican primary sent a strong message to George Bush, which his critics said he ignored. The primary has set virtual political unknowns on their way to the presidency, as it did in 1976 with Jimmy

Christos Spirou (far right), a Greek immigrant who was chairman of the New Hampshire Democratic Party in 1992, leads the applause at a January candidate debate for the five Democratic presidential contenders: (from left) Senator Bob Kerrey of Nebraska, Senator Tom Harkin of Iowa, former Governor Jerry Brown of California, Governor Bill Clinton of Arkansas and former Senator Paul Tsongas of Massachusetts. (Photo by Evan Richman, *Boston Globe*.)

Carter. It has dashed the hopes of many presidential "wannabes" including Senator Edward M. Kennedy in 1980, who as a senator from the next-door state of Massachusetts challenged a sitting president of his own party. It signaled serious problems for Walter F. Mondale in 1984 when he lost in a landslide to Gary Hart. In 1988, it helped George Bush right his topsy-turvy campaign after losing the Iowa caucuses to Senator Bob Dole of Kansas.

With Iowa deemed inconsequential in 1992, New Hampshire assumed even more importance than usual. All of the candidates and the national press corps descended upon the small state towards the end of 1991, although the serious campaigning did not really begin until after the new year. Between January 1 and February 18, primary day, the presidential campaign held the state's voters under siege. The voters of New Hampshire were in a grumpy, skeptical, and worried frame of mind. The state economy, like that of the entire New England region, was in a deep recession. In addition to the less-skilled workers who are always more vulnerable during an economic downturn, many middle managers and white-collar workers with college degrees had lost their jobs. Foreclosure signs on houses were more common than the red, white, and blue signs advertising presidential candidates. Times were tough, and New Hampshire voters were not looking for a cheap thrill in 1992; they wanted serious answers from the people who wanted to be president. More and more began listening to a serious, earnest, almost dour man from Massachusetts named Paul Tsongas.

PAUL TSONGAS ENTERS THE RACE

When Paul Tsongas decided to run for president in 1991, he called his twin sister Thaleia Tsongas Schlesinger and asked her to come to his law office in downtown Boston. When she arrived, he announced that he was going to run against George Bush. He had been out of public life for seven years, but she never blinked an eye. "Well," she said, "you might as well because no one else will say it the way you will." In March of 1991, not a single candidate had yet challenged Bush who appeared to be invincible to the political pros. While Tsongas' twin sister reacted in a matter-of-fact way because she believed in her brother, the reaction of the political establishment ranged from bemused to bewildered. What in the world did Tsongas think he was doing? they wondered aloud. The Democratic party was still smarting from the defeat of Michael Dukakis just three years earlier. The last thing the pundits thought the Democrats needed in 1992 was another liberal Greek candidate from Massachusetts.

Tsongas, a former United States congressman and senator, was, like Dukakis, the son of Greek immigrants. His parents came to the United States when they were young in search of a better life and settled in Lowell, an old mill city near the New Hampshire border. His mother, a school teacher, died from tuberculosis when he was a small child, and he and his sister were raised by their Greek grandparents and their father Efthemios, who ran a dry cleaning establishment on Gorham Street in Lowell. Tsongas was five years older than Bill Clinton, but he too was inspired by President John F. Kennedy who called upon young people in his inaugural address to ask what they could do for their country and not ask what their country could do for them. When Tsongas graduated from Dartmouth College, he enlisted in the Peace Corps, the civilian volunteer organization established by Kennedy which sent young Americans overseas to help educate people in developing countries. Tsongas loved the Peace Corps. After two years as a volunteer teacher in Ethiopia, a country in Africa, he reenlisted to become a Peace Corps supervisor. After he left the Peace Corps, he attended Yale Law School, and, after earning his law degree, he returned home to Lowell to begin a political career. It was a career that took off with amazing speed and success, beginning with the city election of 1969 when he won the election as a Lowell city councilor. Then, in 1972, he became a Middlesex county commissioner and, then, in 1974, he was elected as the congressman from the fifth Congressional district. In 1978, he challenged a sitting U.S. senator, Edward W. Brooke, and beat him.

This rapid rise stopped abruptly when Tsongas found a lump in his groin in 1983 while taking a shower at his Washington home. The lump turned out to be a symptom of a form of cancer called lymphoma, a cancer of the lymph nodes. He was only 42 years old and the father of three young daughters. The news devastated him. He feared that he would die and not see his children grow up just as his mother had died young in a tuberculosis sanitarium in Vermont.

While doctors assured Tsongas that this form of cancer was treatable and he could run for reelection to the Senate in 1984, the cancer diagnosis prompted a period of soul-searching and reflection in the ambitious politician. Forced to confront his own mortality, Tsongas decided that there were more important things in life than being a senator, things like spending more time with his wife Niki and his three daughters, Ashley, Katina, and Molly. He decided not to seek reelection and retired from the Senate. After he left publi? office, the doctors at the Dana Farber Cancer Institute in Boston d?cided to try an experimental treatment on him, a bone marrow transplant, to rid him of the cancer. It appeared to work.

Tsongas had been cancer-free for several years and working as a lawyer in Boston when he began to fret about the state of the nation. The mounting federal debt was an unacceptable burden to future generations he said. He decided that he had to do something about it, at the very least alert the public to the danger of deficit spending and allowing the nation's manufacturing jobs to go overseas. He called it "the obligation of my survival," and despite widespread skepticism, he announced his candidacy on April 30, 1991, in his home town of Lowell.Tsongas became the first truth teller of the 1992 campaign.

Months before he decided to seek the presidency himself, Tsongas sat at his word processor and wrote out a treatise on his notion of the Democratic party's mission in the 1992 presidential campaign. It was 81 pages long and savagely indicted the nation's political leadership for following "feel good" policies and allowing the United States economy to deteriorate, leaving a mountain of debt for their children and grandchildren. It became the policy blueprint for his campaign. Tsongas titled it "A Call to Economic Arms" and turned it into a slim paperback book. He said that the country had to face facts, suck in its collective gut, pay higher taxes on gasoline, and adopt a national industrial policy that targeted tax incentives to business to bring back the well-paying manufacturing jobs. "I want to be the economic Paul Revere," he said, harkening back to another Massachusetts man who had ridden his horse at the start of the U.S. Revolution through the countryside to warn the citizenry that the British soldiers were coming. "I intend to sound the alarm that America must change its national policies to compete."

CLINTON'S STORMY BEGINNING

"Read my book," Tsongas urged audiences in New Hampshire. The worried voters did and liked what they read. Once voters began paying attention to the campaign, Tsongas and Clinton drew the most support in public opinion polls. But from the start, Tsongas' support was more solid. People who decided to back Tsongas were less likely to abandon him for another candidate. Clinton, however, was the attractive newcomer with a message of change and renewal who made Democratic hearts beat a little bit faster. In the charisma contest, he beat Tsongas hands down. Clinton was rapidly becoming the candidate to beat. He moved ahead of Tsongas in public opinion polls in January, held a polling lead of about 12 percentage points, and was featured on the cover of *Time* Magazine as the Democrats' rising star. But then disaster struck the Clinton campaign when a failed cabaret singer named Gennifer Flowers sold a story to a supermarket tabloid newspaper that claimed she had had a 12-year love affair with the married Clinton.

The Flowers Allegations

The news hit New Hampshire on a stormy Thursday, January 16, with the release of advance copies of the supermarket tabloid, *The Star*. The allegations set off a frenzy in the media and threatened to irreparably damage Clinton's candidacy. At that point, Clinton was not very well known outside of his home state of Arkansas. If the first thing that voters learned about him was that he broke his marriage vows, then they might never give him serious consideration. Others who were only interested but not strongly committed to his candidacy might throw him over for another candidate whom they felt they could trust more. To confront these allegations and settle the storm, Clinton and his wife Hillary appeared on the CBS Sunday night show "60 Minutes" and discussed their marriage. They taped an interview with CBS reporter Steve Kroft in a room at the Ritz Carlton Hotel in Boston on Sunday afternoon. Clinton admitted that he had caused pain in his marriage, but he denied that he had been involved with Flowers. She held a press conference in Manhattan the next day and accused him of lying.

The Vietnam Issue

If Gennifer Flowers was not bad enough, another controversial issue popped up almost immediately. During the war in Vietnam, young draft-eligible men, such as Clinton, who opposed the war anguished over the prospect of fighting a war that they considered wrong, misguided, and immoral. Clinton, like many of his generation, used the system of draft deferments given to college students to postpone military service while attending school. The system was not fair because more affluent Americans were using the system to avoid military service while the less well-to-do young men who could not afford to attend college ended up being drafted and sent to Vietnam. So the system was changed. Under the new system, young men would be drafted by birthdates in the order in which the dates were pulled in a lottery. Bill Clinton lucked out and his birthdate was so high on the list that he was never drafted. A *Wall Street Journal* article suggested he had maneuvered his way out of the draft in 1969.

The Character Issue

Gennifer Flowers and the draft story represented a one-two punch for the Clinton campaign because both raised questions about his character. Presidential character had become an increasingly important issue in presidential campaigns. Historians and others said that scrutiny of a candidate's character might have headed off some disastrous policies had the American people known in time. They suggested that the war in Vietnam might not have been escalated had voters known of President Johnson's penchant for lying. The Watergate scandal might have been avoided had voters known of President Nixon's devious and secretive side. By 1992, the press was sensitive to character issues and probed each candidate's background for clues that might give insight into presidential behavior.

Clinton's Comeback

A week before the New Hampshire primary election, Clinton was trailing Tsongas by 11 percentage points in the polls. The political situation was deteriorating for Clinton, but he vowed to fight on. At an Elks Club in Dover on the New Hampshire seacoast, he went before an audience and told them why he was running for presidency. "They say I'm on the ropes because other people have questioned my life, after years of public service," he said. "I'll tell you something—I'm going to give you this election back, and if you'll give it to me, I won't be like George Bush. I'll never forget who gave me a second chance, and I'll be there for you till the last dog dies." Later that night, he again used television to confront the accusations. This time the show was ABC's Nightline. Clinton sat quietly while Ted Koppel, the show host, read the text of an extraordinary letter that Clinton had written 22 years earlier to the head of the ROTC program at the University of Arkansas explaining why he opposed the war and the draft. In the letter, he thanked the military officer for saving him from the draft, proving in a sense the allegations that he had deliberately evaded military service, but the letter also put the draft issue into the perspective of the times, giving insight into a young man's struggle with his conscience.

Clinton spent the final five days of the New Hampshire campaign crisscrossing the state in a relentless attempt to talk to as many voters as he could. He began to climb back in the polls, helped by the inexplicable decision of Tsongas to lay low and barely campaign during the final week of the campaign. Tsongas won the New Hampshire primary, but Clinton finished a strong second. More important, he went on television first that night and declared himself "The Comeback Kid." This strategy created the perception that there were two winners of the New Hampshire primary, Tsongas and Clinton. Up until that time no candidate who had ever lost the New Hampshire primary had been elected president. No one knew it at the time but that bit of political mythology bit the dust that night.

THE REPUBLICANS IN NEW HAMPSHIRE: BUCHANAN'S CHALLENGE

On the Republican side, Patrick J. Buchanan, the syndicated newspaper columnist and pugnacious television co-host of Crossfire on CNN, was mixing for a fight with George Bush. Bush chose to ignore him. Bush ended up regretting that tactic later in the season. To Pat Buchanan, his campaign was a crusade for nothing less than the heart and soul of the Republican party.

Buchanan had grown up as one of nine children, the third son in a Scotch-Irish Catholic family in Washington, D.C. As long as he could remember, he had always been deeply conservative and extremely combative. As a young man, he drank a lot of beer and got into a lot of fights. One night when stopped by police for speeding, Buchanan started fighting with the police officers. He was arrested for resisting arrest and suspended from college for a year. Eleven years later while he was writing speeches on law and order in the White House for Vice President Spiro T. Agnew, a reporter called him to ask if the story was true. With characteristic

While his rival Pat Buchanan toured unemployment offices, President Bush visited only successful businesses on his first campaign trip to New Hampshire in 1992. (Photo courtesy of the Bush Presidential Materials Project of the National Archives.)

candor and lack of remorse, he sighed heavily and said, "I was ahead on points—until they brought out the sticks."

Buchanan was not only colorful, but he was also a credible conservative who had earned his spurs as a speech writer and adviser to three presidents, Nixon, Ford, and Reagan. During the Reagan presidency, he worked in an office just yards away from the office of Vice President Bush. In New Hampshire he charged that George Bush had sold out the Reagan Revolution. In early January, he appeared before the Exeter Rotary Club luncheon at the Exeter Inn. "We can no longer say it is all the liberals fault," he told these Republican businessmen. "It was not a liberal Democrat who said 'Read my lips' and then raised taxes. It was not Teddy Kennedy who said I will not sign the quota bill and then signed the quota bill. You folks saved the nomination for him four years ago. When George Bush said 'Thank you' New Hampshire, he meant goodbye and good luck."

Buchanan was just warming up. "George Bush is the biggest spender in American history," he said. "He is the highest taxer in American history. . . . Jack Kemp said if we elected George Bush the Reagan Revolution is dead. He was right." This last shot was a tough one because Kemp, a Bush opponent for the Republican presidential nomination in 1988, was by then a member of the Bush cabinet as secretary of Housing and Urban Development. Kemp, like Buchanan, was also a hero to conservatives. Buchanan had almost no chance of wresting the party nomination from an incumbent president because the Republican party rules flagrantly favored the incumbent. But as a credible conservative critic, he gave voice to many Republican concerns about Bush and his performance. While Bush refused to even utter Buchanan's name, the motley Buchanan campaign traveled the highways and backroads of New Hampshire in a silver Plymouth Voyager van and chipped away day by day at the President's standing in the state.

The Bush Response

Bush did not help his own cause. For most of the New Hampshire campaign he let stand-ins known as "surrogates," such as his wife Barbara and New Hampshire Governor Judd Gregg, who was the chairman of his state campaign, represent him in the

Barbara Bush, the popular First Lady, stopped by a Bush-Quayle campaign office to call voters and urge them to vote for her husband. (Photo courtesy of the Bush Presidential Materials Project of the National Archives.)

state. He went to Japan on a trade mission and in an unfortunate incident vomited at a state dinner. On his first campaign trip to the state, Bush did little to improve his image. His campaign advisers had told him that the message of the trip was to convince New Hampshire voters that he cared about them. So he blurted out, "Message: I care." Not only did he fail to make a compelling case for a second term for himself, but he did not give people the answers they wanted to financial problems involving job security and health care coverage.

President Bush came from a patrician background. During the Great Depression when millions of Americans were out of work, he was chauffeured to school by a family driver. His father was a wealthy U.S. senator from Connecticut. Although many wealthy Americans have been effective and beloved leaders in the United States, Bush's background worked against him because he seemed out of touch with the lives and fears of average people. Early in February, he went to a grocery trade show in Orlando, Florida, and expressed astonishment at a display featuring an electronic supermarket scanner, an item that had been in common use for more than ten years in grocery stores across the nation. In politics, a picture can be worth thousands of words and that picture of Bush expressing amazement at an everyday device reinforced the sense that he did not understand the concerns of average Americans. In politics, that sort of perception can be deadly because people expect their leaders to understand them.

THE RESULTS OF THE NEW HAMPSHIRE PRIMARY

President Bush and Tsongas won their respective primary contests in New Hampshire as expected. When politicians meet expectations, they often do not get credit they deserve for winning. Although Bush beat Buchanan handily by a margin that would

Pat Buchanan met the press the morning after the New Hampshire primary with a big smile and the morning paper with its front page message to President Bush: "Read Our Lips." (Photo by Bill Greene, *Boston Globe.*)

constitute a landslide by any normal reckoning, he drew less than 50 percent of all Republican votes that day after all the write-in votes were counted. When an incumbent president has half of all voters of his own party voting for someone else, it is seen as a vote of "no confidence." Bush was off to a rocky start. Buchanan viewed his better-than-expected showing as a victory. He crowed: "From dawn to dusk, the Buchanan brigades met King George's army all along the Concord-Manchester-Nashua line, and I am here to report they are retreating back into Massachusetts."

Tsongas beat Clinton by nine percentage points, a handsome win, but Clinton scored points politically by fighting back from setbacks that might have undone another candidacy. Kerrey only received 12 percent of the vote and Harkin 11 percent. It seemed clear that they would be out of the race very soon. In fact, Kerrey withdrew on March 4, and Harkin followed five days later on March 9. While Brown only got 9 percentage points, his situation was different because he was not running to win so much as he was running to make a point. His unusual low budget campaign could keep on going so long as Brown—Energizer-Bunny style—kept on

President Bush's first campaign trip to New Hampshire did little to draw new support, but it may have shored up his loyalists in the first primary state. (Photo courtesy of the Bush Presidential Materials Project of the National Archives.)

going. Few commentators took him seriously at that point, but his appeal would prove itself within a week at the presidential caucuses in Maine, the frosty state next door.

After months in New Hampshire, the campaigns all packed up and moved towards the South where the next big contests were scheduled to take place. The retail phase of the campaign acted as the initial test market for the presidential candidates. Candidates showed their wares to a discerning slice of the electorate who selectively picked what they liked and discarded the rest. The successful candidates with the resources and support to continue in the campaign had also sharpened and focused their messages. The campaign and the survivors were now ready to move into the wholesale phase.

Chapter 4

Getting It Wholesale: Using the Media to Reach a Mass Audience

The day after a primary election is like the day a circus or carnival pulls up its stakes, collapses its tent, and leaves town for the next stop on the road show. The candidates, their campaign staff, and the national press corps fly away to the state with the next contest. A few members of the campaign field staff stay behind to dismantle the campaign headquarters. They pack up signs that can be used again; store the precious lists of voters' names, addresses, and voting history; and stuff position papers and brochures into cardboard boxes. The exhausted volunteers return to their normal lives. The local news broadcasts abruptly shift from presidential candidate pronouncements to local fires and crimes. Within hours, the campaign headquarters is transformed from a throbbing command center into abandonned office space. All that remains are a few coffee cups; a ripped red, white, and blue wall sign; and overflowing trash barrels. Miles away in another state, the campaign ground troops, the "grunts" of politics, drive stakes into the ground to set up another temporary operational center for another relentless run to election day.

SUPER TUESDAY

But after New Hampshire, there is one important difference. Most conventional campaigns try to establish a presence on the ground in each caucus or primary state to coordinate a local campaign and give the local voters a sense that they want their votes—"a field campaign" in campaign parlance. But after the New Hampshire primary, most of the candidate's money, thought, and effort goes into "the air war"—the battle fought over the television and radio airwaves. The campaign calendar brings about this shift in tactics because the candidates move from competing in one small state at one time to competing in many states at the same time. A candidate can drive from one end of New Hampshire to the other in a matter of hours. New Hampshire is a manageable environment for campaigns because the state contains only 1.1 million residents and has only one local commercial television station, WMUR-TV in Manchester, Channel 9.

On Tuesday, March 10, 1992, 11 separate elections in 11 different states from Texas to Tennessee and from Florida to Massachusetts took place at the same time. Most of those contests took place in the South, part of the so-called Super Tuesday primary. Super Tuesday was the scheme cooked up by a group of moderate Southern Democrats after the Mondale loss in 1984. They reasoned that if all or most of the Southern states held their primary contests on the same day, then a more moderate (hopefully Southern) presidential candidate would be helped because that is the type of candidate who theoretically did best in their states. These politicians, most of them state legislators, were tired of the Democratic party always losing presidential elections. If the party nominated a more moderate candidate, someone more like them, instead of a liberal from the Midwest or Northeast like Walter Mondale or Michael Dukakis, they thought their chances of victory in November would improve.

This strategy backfired in 1988 because Jesse L. Jackson, the only black candidate in the race, Senator Albert Gore, Jr., of Tennessee, the only southern candidate, and Michael S. Dukakis, the eventual nominee, split the total vote. This split vote muddied the results and no one emerged as a clear and unquestioned "dragon slayer" on that day. In 1992, Super Tuesday worked the way its originators had hoped and benefited the candidacy of Bill Clinton.

The Logistics of Super Tuesday

Political strategy aside, Super Tuesday posed a daunting logistical challenge to any candidate because no candidate, no matter how hard working or well organized, can spend enough time in each Super Tuesday state to run an effective campaign. Radio and television advertisements and appearances become critically important to expand the candidate's presence across larger geographic areas. During the Super Tuesday phase of the campaign the candidates conduct "tarmac campaigning" by flying from airport to airport and holding press conferences. For example, a Pat Buchanan press conference at the Tulsa airport terminal would be covered by local television and newspaper reporters. Their reports would take Buchanan's messages to hundreds of thousands of people even though Buchanan did not have the time to talk to a single real voter in Tulsa.

The candidate with the most money to purchase television time enjoys a distinct advantage. Bush had a built-in advantage over Buchanan because as the incumbent president he could command instant and comprehensive news coverage at any moment. Although Paul Tsongas won the New Hampshire primary and got the anticipated boost of momentum from that victory, his campaign had been living hand to mouth from the beginning. The influx of contributions that came with his victory did not come in time to catch up to the head start that Clinton had in the South. For the Georgia presidential primary on March 3, Clinton not only had the support of key local politicians including the state's popular governor, Zell Miller, but he had more money to spend on the local campaign. By contrast, Tsongas' campaign in Georgia just days before that important contest consisted of a telephone answering machine in Atlanta.

PRESIDENTIAL CAMPAIGNS AND TELEVISION SINCE 1960

Presidential politics entered the media age during the 1960 presidential campaign with the first televised presidential debate between John F. Kennedy and Richard M. Nixon. Kennedy, the Democratic presidential candidate, was a U.S. senator from Massachusetts. Nixon, a former U.S. senator from California, served as vice president to Dwight D. Eisenhower, the World War II general who had been the Republican president for the previous eight years. The 1960 presidential campaign was the first one to take place in what could really be considered a television age. Black-and-white television sets first entered the households of Americans in large numbers during the 1950s. Color TV's arrived on the scene much later.

At first, candidates were unskilled and clumsy at this new medium. In the pre-television age, even before the days of radio, a candidate's ability to deliver eloquent speeches and deliver his message by word was important. Back in the earliest days of the United States, newspapers would publish the entire text of politicians' speeches, but months might elapse before a voter would even have an opportunity to read it. It was still important to be able to persuade people to a certain point of view with an intellectual reasoned argument, but television was a different animal, a visual animal, which put a premium on appearance. The substance of a candidate's words could be overwhelmed by the way he or she looked. Television introduced a whole new set of considerations to political campaigns. The wrong necktie or a big hat could totally distract viewers from the candidate's message or even convey the wrong impression. During the 1992 campaign, Frank Greer, Bill Clinton's top media consultant, advised him to wear nothing but red-striped ties. Clinton preferred more colorful ties with interesting prints and patterns, but he followed his consultant's advice because the sober stripes conveyed a more serious style appropriate for a would-be president. For all the potential risks of television, politicians also recognized the potential power of the television camera to convey a message to millions of voters at the same time.

The Checkers Speech

Nixon used television to get himself out of a political jam after Eisenhower picked him to be his vice president in 1952. Questions were raised about a $18,235 political fund that his supporters in California had raised for his personal use. Campaign finance laws were not as strict then as now, but Eisenhower thought the fund sounded dubious, and he considered throwing the young U.S.

senator off the presidential ticket and replacing him with someone else. To save his political career, Nixon took to the television. He hired an advertising agency to stage a broadcast. For 30 minutes, with his wife Pat sitting behind him, he explained why he needed this fund to pay his living expenses. Nixon did not come from a wealthy family, and he spoke about his mortgaged home, his wife's cloth coat, and admitted that a supporter had given a dog, Checkers, to his little girls, Julie and Tricia. No way was he going to take Checkers away from his daughters he said. The speech went down in political lore as "the Checkers speech." His performance, watched by millions of Americans, generated public sympathy for him. Nixon saved himself. Eisenhower kept him on the ticket.

The presidential seal on the front of his bulletproof podium conveyed the authority and prestige of his office for President Bush, especially on television. (Photo courtesy of the Bush Presidential Materials Project of the National Archives.)

Fireside Chats on Television?

The impact of television can really be seen when thinking about how historical figures might have been affected by the medium. Franklin D. Roosevelt delivered fireside chats from the White House that were conveyed to millions of households on the radio during World War II. The president had been disabled by polio, a disease that crippled millions before the discovery of a preventive vaccine, and he was confined to a wheelchair. At the time, most Americans did not know this because the press corps did not report it. His rich, reassuring voice reached as many as 60 million Americans for 27 fireside chats over six years; these broadcasts were so memorable that many people who were alive then still think today that they took place every single week.

The fancy, new medium of television began to make its presence felt during the Truman administration. Vice President Harry S. Truman became president when Roosevelt died in 1945, only one month into his fourth term. Truman was elected in his own right in 1948 to a four-year term. The first telecast from the White House took place when Truman announced the Food Conservation Program. The first presidential news conference was broadcast on TV during the administration of Dwight D. Eisenhower in 1955. It was taped because Ike never allowed live broadcasts of his news conferences. His staff feared he might make a mistake on the air.

The Kennedy-Nixon Debate

By 1960, television had become a common household appliance in the United States. In 1950, only 11 percent or 4.4 million households owned a television set. Just ten years later, about 40 million households owned televisions, more than 88 percent of all American families. The two very modern men seeking the presidency that year, John Kennedy and Richard Nixon, were more comfortable with television than Truman or Eisenhower had been. Both Kennedy and Nixon had some experience with TV and valued its power. They agreed to participate in the four televised presidential debates in the fall, a breakthrough in American politics that would set an expectation and a standard for presidential debate that remains in effect today.

The first debate, held in Chicago on September 26, 1960, turned into a political disaster for Nixon. Kennedy won the debate hands down over Nixon and not because Nixon made a mistake on the issues or because Kennedy scored intellectual debating points. Kennedy won because he looked better. Kennedy made sure that he would be rested for the encounter. He arrived in Chicago a full day before the debate was scheduled to air and stayed in a hotel suite lying on his back in bed, fielding questions from his staff. He had picked up a light tan, which made him look better on television. He also took a two-hour nap before the debate. By contrast, Nixon showed up for the encounter exhausted and still recovering from sickness. He had been hospitalized earlier in the month for nearly two weeks at Walter Reed Hospital with a serious knee infection. By the time the debate took place, he had still not fully recovered. Nixon seemed snake bitten. He banged his sore knee on a car door on his way into the studio. Sweat streaked the type of make-up he used called Lazy Shave, which was supposed to cover his five o'clock shadow. The television camera exaggerated the hollows and lines of his face, showing plainly Nixon's fatigue and strain. While Nixon sweat profusely under the hot television lights, Kennedy looked cool, calm, and collected.

The first impression would prove to be the lasting one. While Nixon recovered somewhat in the three subsequent debates, (he even used theatrical makeup to improve his appearance on television) the damage had been done before 70 million viewers. The election results of 1960 were the closest in history. Kennedy received 49.7 percent of the vote to Nixon's 49.6 percent. Nixon and generations of politicians who followed him blamed his debate appearance for the loss by 112,881 out of almost 69 million votes cast.

THE ROLE OF COMMERCIALS

When Nixon made his political comeback in 1968—this time successfully—he remembered the lessons from the 1960 campaign. In the 1968 campaign he attempted to control the television pictures of himself. In politics there are two types of television exposure, "free" and "paid." Free time is the television time that comes on television talk and interview shows, on debates, and in the news broadcasts. Paid media are the 30- and 60-second commercials that are aired on time purchased by the campaigns. In 1992, several candidates, particularly Ross Perot, popularized the so-called infomercial—a full half hour of purchased time to deliver a long issue-oriented campaign message.

The first television commercials were aired for Eisenhower in the 1956 campaign, but they were little more than radio jingles with photographs. Nixon brought paid media to a new height of political sophistication in 1968 with staged town meetings that featured a panel of hand-picked questioners. These forums allowed Nixon to appear intelligent, presidential, and in command before friendly audiences. The forums, called "the man in the arena" by his media consultant, Roger Ailes (the same media consultant who advised George Bush in his presidential campaign 20 years later), were the first use of television in a campaign to create an illusion of reality in a way that protected the candidate from error or embarrassment. The forums presented a Nixon who seemed to be a reassuring figure, a leader who could be trusted. This image provided a stark contrast to the disarray and confusion, the tear gas, and rioting outside the Democratic Convention that had nominated Hubert Humphrey that year. Nixon learned to use television to package himself in a way that was attractive to voters.

In the last 25 years, television has become so important that TV advertising time and production now consume most of a candidate's campaign budget. Even Iowa and New Hampshire, the retail states, have entered the media age. Although many more voters in New Hampshire have the opportunity to meet a candidate in person and even question him or her about issues in a neighbor's living room over chocolate chip cookies, in practice, most voters get their information about the candidates and the campaign from radio, television, and the newspapers. TV ads are used to reinforce the candidate's message and exploit voter sentiments to benefit a candidacy. Patrick Buchanan's most often aired television ad in the 1992 New Hampshire campaign used a snippet of tape from George Bush's 1988 convention speech in which Bush, Clint Eastwood-style, said, "Read my lips . . . no new taxes." Bush broke his promise and entered into a budget agreement with Congress that raised taxes. Buchanan cleverly used Bush's own words against him.

Later in the year, Clinton would use the same piece of tape to make the same point about Bush's trustworthiness. The Buchanan "Read My Lips" ad aired so often in New Hampshire that little preschoolers were bawling "Read my lips" to their friends at day-care centers, evidence that the ad had reached saturation levels of coverage and the message had got through even to children who may not have quite understood its meaning.

THE FIRST ADS OF 1992

The first ad in a political campaign is often used to introduce the candidate to people who know little or nothing about him or her. Ads can also convey an impression, educate voters about a position or issue, or fix an image problem. Paul Tsongas was better known in New Hampshire than Clinton or the other candidates because he lived just a few miles over the border and had served as a senator from the neighboring state of Massachusetts whose television stations were watched by residents of the Granite State. But some voters who agreed with him on the issues were hesitant to support him because of his bout with cancer. They feared he might be physically unable to serve as president. The job of president is a hard and stressful one and has caused all of the modern presidents to age rapidly while in office. The before and after pictures of Jimmy Carter and George Bush show men with far more wrinkles and gray hair after four years in office. If a president dies in office, the U.S. Constitution provides for the vice president to automatically become president. Although this provision guarantees a rapid and peaceful transition of power, the death of a president is a national trauma whether by natural means or by an assassin's bullet.

The president's health has become a bigger issue in recent years as historians have discovered medical facts about long dead presidents that were not known when those presidents were alive and serving the country. The fact that Franklin D. Roosevelt could not even stand without assistance because of the ravages of polio was not known by most Americans during his lifetime. John Kennedy not only had a chronic back problem, but he also suffered from Addison's' disease and took a lot of medication to control it, which voters did not know. Some people feel that public figures are entitled to a little bit of privacy, particularly about personal health or their children. Others say that the public right to know covers anything that affects a president's ability to perform his duties.

The Tsongas Ads

To deal with the public concern about his medical condition, Tsongas' first ad showed him vigorously swimming laps in an Olympic-sized pool. Wearing only his Speedo, the 50-year-old Tsongas looked pretty fit. Tsongas had another political problem, however. Many Democrats were worried that he was so quiet and low key that he would be unable to win the election in November. In politics, a characteristic that is detrimental to the candidacy is

Paul Tsongas, the first cancer survivor to ever seek the presidency, tried to ease voter concerns about his health in his commercials by appearing in a Speedo bathing suit and goggles and swimming vigorously. (Photo by John Tlumacki, *Boston, Globe.*)

called "a negative." For Tsongas, his willingness to talk about the tough issues was considered "a positive" in the environment of 1992, but his lack of charisma was considered "a negative." To deal with this particular negative, his campaign advisers Fred Woods and Michael Shea produced a 30-second ad called "Leadership."

The ad began with a commentator saying, "He's no movie star, but Paul Tsongas is something else." Political advisers had learned that it is better to acknowledge reality because the public is not stupid and would resent it if the campaign people tried to claim Tsongas was charismatic like a movie star when it was obvious to anyone who knew him that he was a pretty low-key person.

As the video showed, in succession, images of Tsongas at a podium, in an auto assembly plant, and with workers, the commentator intoned: "When no one thought Chrysler could survive, it was Paul Tsongas who forced the agreement in Congress that saved 100,000 jobs."

The images changed to an aerial shot of Alaska and another picture of Tsongas as the commentator continued: "When special interest were grabbing up our last great wilderness, Paul Tsongas pushed through what has been called the 'conservation bill of the century.'"

The screen then flashed a headline that said, "Bush's popularity surges to 90 percent" as the commentator said, "And while others feared the president's popularity, Paul Tsongas took him on and offered a new economic vision for America."

The ad closed with a picture of Tsongas speaking and a commentator saying, "Getting the tough jobs done, it's called leadership."

In 30 quick seconds, this ad confronted a voter concern about Tsongas' potential lack of appeal by acknowledging that he is no movie star and by pointing to his record in the Senate to show that he had saved workers' jobs and protected the environment. It also suggested that he was not afraid to take chances and do what he thought was right despite long odds.

Tom Harkin's Ads

The most emotional ads were produced for Senator Tom Harkin by Ken Swope, a Boston adman. One featured the empty

Pandora Mills in Manchester, New Hampshire, where generations of New Hampshire workers had labored, producing sweaters and sportswear. The business had closed because of foreign competition throwing hundreds out of work. Harkin is shown speaking inside this cavernous mill, "You can look down this hallway, you can hear the echoes of people who once worked here. What I hear when I hear these echoes is a challenge to us, not to forget what makes this country the great, wonderful America that we are. People at work, and what they are saying to us. Don't forget. Don't give up. Build it again. We can do it." Harkin's ads with their stirring music pulled at the heart strings, but they could not convince enough people to vote for him. Voters did not want a blast from the past, which was the basic pitch of this old-fashioned liberal, but someone or something new and different. Voters wanted change.

Bob Kerrey's Ads

Like Harkin, Bob Kerrey's campaign never quite got off the ground in New Hampshire even though Kerrey was considered a political consultant's dream of the ideal candidate. Not only was he a baby boomer like Clinton, but he was also a war hero. He had a charming personality and that spark of something special called charisma. Kerrey also had served as governor of his state of Nebraska before winning election to the U.S. Senate, so experience was not a problem. His top issue was health care. One of voter's biggest concerns was being able to get good, affordable health care. With the population aging, many voters were having a difficult time caring for elderly parents and worried about how their own health care needs would be met when they grew old themselves. An interest group called New Hampshire Asks chased candidates all over the state with signs that asked: "How is a family that makes $35,000 a year supposed to pay $30,000 a year for grandma's long term care?" It was a good question, and Kerrey was one of the candidates who tried to answer it.

But Kerrey turned out to be a somewhat lackluster candidate. A lot of political professionals wondered if he really wanted to be president. When his health care message did not seem to be pushing him up in the public opinion polls, he shifted to the issue of foreign competition and taped a television ad in a hockey rink that was criticized for bashing foreign competitors and not addressing adequately the problems in U.S. industry. He ended up agreeing that the ad was a mistake.

The Ineffectiveness of Commercials in 1992

The importance of campaign ads reached a peak in 1988 when George Bush used television ads to convince voters that Michael Dukakis was an unacceptably risky liberal. One famous ad showed a turnstile at a prison gate with prisoners going in and out to deliver the message that Dukakis was soft on crime. Another ad showed pollution in Boston's famous harbor and blamed Dukakis for the mess. But four years later, both the media and the public were more skeptical. Voters were so angry and worried about the economy that they wanted more substance and more answers from politicians. A warm and wonderful scene or a scary image in a TV ad was no longer enough to make most support or reject a candidacy.

USE OF MEDIA IN THE 1992 CAMPAIGN

Radio Talk Shows

The 1992 campaign opened a new chapter for the use of television and radio in a presidential campaign. Necessity was the mother of this strategy. None of the challengers had much money. While Clinton started the year with campaign receipts of $3 million, the most of any Democratic candidate, four years earlier Michael Dukakis had raised more than three times that amount in the same period of time. Because none of the challengers had a lot of cash, they were forced to be creative and seek out opportunities for free exposure on television and radio. The proliferation of talk radio shows created inviting forums for candidates to stop by and chat for awhile and take voters' telephone calls on the air. All of the challengers used talk radio early and often in the campaign, particularly Jerry Brown.

Television Talk Shows

Television also entered the act. Larry King had a call-in show on Cable News Network. He invited the Texas businessman Ross Perot to appear on his television show on February 20 and asked him why he wouldn't run for president. The question was a plant from John Jay Hooker, a sharp Tennessee politician who had been urging Perot to run for president since November. Hooker thought that Perot could be the Eisenhower of his generation. After months of coaxing, Perot said he might consider it if his name got on the ballot in all 50 states. Hooker encouraged Larry King to ask this question on the air. When Perot gave the same answer that he had given Hooker, it was as if he had flicked a lit match into an open can of gasoline. His response started a national movement. That night Perot returned to his suite at the Hay-Adams hotel just across Lafayette Park from the White House and assured his wife, Margot, that nothing would come of his comments. Moments later, an anonymous donor pushed a $5 bill under the door with a note encouraging him to run. The next day his office telephones in Dallas nearly rang off the hook, and within days petition drives to get him on the ballot were underway in 46 states. The candidacy of Ross Perot took on a life of its own after that first appearance on Larry King Live.

ROSS PEROT

From the beginning, Perot was different from the other presidential candidates. He could skip the retail phase when candidates seeking their party nominations attempted to persuade individual voters one at a time to support their candidacies. Instead, Perot took his message to the masses of people, directly and immediately, via television without first conducting the "test marketing" among small groups of voters in the early testing grounds of Iowa and New Hampshire. In this way, Perot's campaign in 1992 was the ultimate television campaign. Indeed, every major moment in the Perot campaign took place before a television camera. His campaign commercials were one of the crucial ways he communicated with the American people.

Many political observers believe that the most effective political ads of the year were the starkly simple ones produced for Ross Perot when he finally entered the race in October. The ads were all 60 seconds long and featured words scrolling down a screen while an authoritative, deep-voiced commentator, who sounded like God, spoke. The ads addressed the issue that voters were most concerned about: the state of the economy. A Perot ad called "Our Children" showed words scrolling over a magnified, close-up picture of a smiling child. The commentator said:

> Our children dream of the world that we promise them as parents, a world of unlimited opportunity. What would they say to us if they knew that, by the year 2000, we will have left them with a national debt of $8 trillion? What would they say to us if they knew that we are making them the first generation of Americans with a standard of living below the generation before them? We cannot do this to our children. In this election, we have the opportunity to choose a candidate who is not a career politician but a proven business leader with the ability to take on the tasks at hand, to balance the budget, to expand the tax base, to give our children back their American dream. The candidate is Ross Perot. The issue is our children. The choice is yours.

Perot's Use of Television

In 1992, Perot used television better than any other presidential candidate to reach and educate voters. Perot was a master salesman. He used television to not only sell himself but also sell his ideas about improving the U.S. economy. Perot was not a conventional presidential candidate. He had never held public office, nor had he ever run for public office. This type of candidate is unusual in the American political system. Most presidential candidates have served as governors or members of congress or senators, often for many years, and most have a lot of experience in electoral politics searching for votes. But Perot was a businessman who made billions of dollars in the computer service industry. He was a real American folk hero, a maverick entrepreneur who did things his way or no way. He looked like the opposite of the tall, handsome, blow-dried politician. He was a small, tough man with a crew cut who had been born in Texarkana, Texas.

Perot's father was a cotton broker and horse trader. Although his family had more money than most during the Depression years when he was growing up, he learned the value of hard work as a boy through a newspaper route and other jobs. He attended the Naval Academy at Annapolis and worked for IBM, the computer giant, in its early years before leaving to establish his own successful businesses. Perot had become known to many Americans as an advocate of American prisoners of war and men missing in action during the war in Vietnam. In his homestate of Texas, he led a crusade to reform the public schools and rid his hometown, Dallas, of drugs. When two of his employees were taken prisoner by revolutionaries in Iran, he organized and financed a SWAT team of soldiers of fortune to break them out of jail.

Perot's Appeal

In 1992, Perot appealed to many people precisely because he was not a politician. He spoke bluntly and persuasively, using anecdotes and folksy phrases to make complicated economic issues crystal clear. After his appearance on Larry King Live on CNN, volunteers who thought that he should run for the presidency began to collect signatures of voters to get his name on the election ballots in every state. Perot said he would not declare his candidacy unless his supporters reached this goal, which involves pouring through complicated election laws and thousands of staff-hours of volunteer labor to collect the valid signatures of registered voters.

For all his money, Perot was a plainspoken and unpretentious man. Once he was scheduled to make a live appearance on one of the network morning shows in October. He drove himself in his Ford Explorer to the network affiliate station in Dallas in the predawn dark. When the technicians checked Perot's microphone to make sure that he could be heard by the interviewer who was in touch by satellite in New York, he recited, "one billion, two billion," and then switched to "one trillion, two trillion," to check the sound. Everyone within earshot cracked up laughing. He also had a huge ego as do most of the men who seek the presidency. As he began to pick up support, he began to attract greater press scrutiny, the scrutiny that all serious candidates for the presidency receive in these times.

Because money was no object, Perot hired some of the best political tacticians in the business including Hamilton Jordan, the Democratic operative from Georgia who had run Jimmy Carter's successful campaign in 1976, and Ed Rollins, the Republican operative from California who had run Ronald Reagan's reelection campaign in 1984. Perot had worked with both Democrats and Republicans over the years, and the fact that he could hire top campaign operatives from both political parties said a lot about his unusual bipartisan appeal to voters. If Clinton was neither liberal nor conservative, then Perot was really a clean slate and for awhile represented all things to all people because few really knew what he believed. As the slate began to fill up with facts and stories from his long business career and his past dabbling in politics, the picture that began to emerge to the public was not completely flattering.

The Response to Perot

By June, when the nominating season ended and Bush and Clinton had their respective nominations in hand, the Perot candidacy was booming, but even before then, his popularity was soaring. By the first week in May, he passed Clinton in national public opinion polls. A week later, he passed Bush. The Bush White House recognized a threat when it saw it and began to criticize Perot. The news media began to take a more penetrating look at this business-man who wanted to be president. The news stories were highly critical. They reported that he had hired private investigators to spy on business rivals and even his own children, that he had tried to cut business deals with the Vietnamese when he traveled to Hanoi ostensibly to secure the release of imprisoned U.S. service men, and that he had avoided paying some taxes and unfairly won some government contracts. Marlin Fitzwater, the president's press secretary, called him a monster. Vice President Dan Quayle described Perot as a temperamental tycoon with no regard for the Constitution.

Perot Leaves the Race

Perot hated the negative publicity. On July 16, he abruptly decided to quit the race. The timing benefited Clinton because

Perot dropped out on the very day that Clinton was to formally accept the Democratic party presidential nomination at the Democratic National Convention in New York City. It also hurt Perot more than he could realize at the time because he was labeled a quitter in the national media and his volunteer supporters were bitterly disappointed at his decision, which he made without consulting with them. This transgression was a fatal error for a candidate who claimed to be totally responsive to the people and his grassroots organization. "He stared American politics in the eye," said one historian at the University of Texas, Lewis L. Gould, "and he blinked." The myth of Ross Perot began to crumble.

CONCLUSION

Television and radio were well positioned to meet the public's demand for more information and more answers from the candidates for president. During the New Hampshire primary campaign, the voters thirst for policy proposals was so strong that several

Bill Clinton understood the importance of television throughout the campaign and, later, for his inaugural address, he kept his speech short to hold the attention of a channel-surfing television audience. (Photo by John Tlumacki, *Boston Globe.*)

candidates followed the lead of Tsongas and put their proposals together in little booklets. The Tsongas campaign printed up more than 200,000 of his *Call to Economic Arms* and distributed them throughout the country. An ad aired in the New Hampshire primary by Clinton urged viewers to call the campaign or visit the local library to obtain a copy of his health care proposal. Thousands did. Ross Perot published a somewhat larger book called *United We Stand: How We Can Take Back Our Country*. Both *United We Stand* and the paperback book containing the proposals of the Democratic ticket, which Clinton and Gore called *Putting People First: How We Can All Change America,* wound up on the best-seller lists.

Television news journalists and the so-called print press, the newspaper and magazine reporters, also attempted during the campaign to produce more stories about issues and fewer stories about campaign tactics and the horse race. The public was in an anti-establishment mood in 1992, and many voters were skeptical about the institutional press and complained that reporters were too interested in personality and tactics. There was some truth to this accusation, but the public also had an insatiable thirst for gossip, and stories about personal scandal sold better than stories about health care proposals.

When reporters cover a national political campaign, they focus on one issue or event at a time and use their best judgment to provide perspective and background so voters understand the issue completely. Many voters did not want the press to filter out anything in 1992 and preferred to get their information themselves by watching the candidates field questions from people like themselves on the television. Later in the year the television morning shows, the "Today Show" on NBC, "Good Morning America" on ABC, and "CBS This Morning," featured the candidates in extended question-and-answer sessions that sometimes consumed the entire two-hour shows. Bill Clinton also used the so-called free media to give the public a better sense of who he was in June, after the nominating season, ended in a blitz of appearances that literally resurrected his candidacy.

The candidates who met and surmounted the logistical challenge of Super Tuesday, George Bush and Bill Clinton, were well on their way to winning their party nominations the day after that March election. In 1992, Super Tuesday finally worked the way its architects had envisioned. It benefited the more moderate candidates and helped those candidates lock up the party nominations well in advance of the nominating conventions.

By the time the wholesale phase of the campaign was over, the public images of the major political candidates for the fall campaign were beginning to solidify for the voters. Initial impressions picked up from reading a newspaper story or magazine article or watching a television commercial or seeing the network news had begun to sketch the outlines in the public mind of the candidates who wanted to be president. If the campaign was a symphony and candidates songwriters, the wholesale phase was the equivalent of producing the first bars of a melody and the musical refrain that would echo back again and again in the fall campaign.

Chapter 5:

On the Trail: The Insurgent Campaign

Pat Buchanan ran a classic insurgent campaign in 1992. Driven by ideology, this man of strong opinion and stronger conviction ignored the odds and challenged a sitting president of his own political party. His rhetoric resonated with restive Republicans. He attracted to his effort a band of hardy, if young and inexperienced, true believers. To make a point, Buchanan persisted long after rational people said he had no chance of winning. As the campaign progressed, his limited resources proved to be an insurmountable obstacle. An examination of Buchanan and his insurgent campaign in the days following the New Hampshire primary in late February 1992 shows the inner workings of a presidential campaign on a typical day.

MODERN CAMPAIGNS

Presidential campaigns have become grueling marathons in modern times. To complete the arduous course, the successful competitors must pace themselves like long-distance runners. By the final sprint to Election Day, the sleep-deprived candidates and their traveling parties are usually cruising on a toxic mix of fatigue, adrenaline, and exhilaration. Any campaign is exhausting, but a presidential campaign becomes mind numbing because of the large number of primary and caucus contests and the geographical sweep of the nation. The candidates, their campaign staffs, and the traveling press corps become strangely isolated from reality during an intense campaign; they live and work together in a surreal campaign environment of chartered jets and hotel rooms for months on end. The real world of monthly bills, family responsibilities, and daily routine fades away. Those on the trail become obsessed with survival. Simple things like clean laundry, a real meal, a hot shower, and, in 1992, a modular telephone for filing stories from lap top computers, become vitally important. In the steel cylinder of the campaign plane—known as "the bus"—reporters and staff alike become fixated by the smallest changes and developments.

PHASE ONE OF THE BUCHANAN CAMPAIGN

During the first phase of Buchanan's campaign, a crusade for what he liked to call "the heart and soul of the Republican Party," he needed nothing more than a roomy minivan to crisscross the small state of New Hampshire. After the New Hampshire primary election, the stakes got higher, the distances longer, and the demands greater. As he headed south, he needed far more than the trusty Plymouth Voyager to compete against Bush in the many contests taking place simultaneously on March 3 (mini-Super Tuesday) and March 10 (Super Tuesday). Bush enjoyed the advantages of the presidency: instant command of media attention, sophisticated military support for travel including Air Force One, the experienced White House advance office to arrange his schedule, and a small army of campaign workers. By contrast, Buchanan left Dulles Airport in suburban Virginia three days after the New Hampshire primary in an old 50-seat Convair turbo prop with a single aide, Greg Mueller, his press secretary, who was a 29-year-old political consultant who was working on his first presidential campaign.

Nonetheless, Buchanan was not without resources. He had "momentum," an intangible political potion that can sometimes transform a long shot into a front-runner if the conditions are exactly right. He had a message—something to say—and the ability to articulate that message. And he had a vulnerable opponent in George Bush. But any objective observer could see the logistical challenge alone was daunting. Buchanan already seemed overextended. His first trip after the New Hampshire primary got off to a late start because the candidate was writing and taping his own campaign commercials at his home in suburban Washington. Mary

Matalin, a high-ranking Bush campaign aide, appeared on a morning television show the day after the New Hampshire primary and tartly dismissed Buchanan's effort: "Whirly birding all over the South is not a campaign," she spat, "it's a book tour."

Buchanan's Challenge in the South

Buchanan needed to demonstrate that his showing in New Hampshire was more than a one-state fluke, the reaction of a disgruntled citizenry in an atypical state with a bad economy. He had never seriously thought he would beat Bush for the presidential nomination, but his better-than-expected showing in New Hampshire had quickened his pulse. He talked about the experience during a quiet moment over coffee in his suite at the Wayfarer Hotel, a hotel in suburban Manchester, New Hampshire, that becomes a home away from home for the national press corps every four years.

> You wouldn't come in here unless you have a dream. You lie awake at night and think "We'll go up to New Hampshire, surprise him, and roll right through the nomination." And other times you wake up at night and say "What do you think you are doing coming from the McLaughlin Group and challenging the president of the United States?" I have had both of these sentiments, tilting at windmills and other times I think it is there. I think there is an army that will rise up.
>
> It is very heartening to me. As late as November 20, this campaign was Bay and me talking on the phone over whether something could be done. And in nine and a half weeks, we have this huge army in New Hampshire. We are matching him ad for ad, dollar for dollar. We have a better organization. You have got all these kids up here. You have the (New York) *Times* saying Bush is nervous. It has been terrific. No matter how it comes out, it has been a wonderful experience.

Secret Service Involvement

Although it is not unusual for a presidential candidate to campaign by himself with only a few volunteers in tow in December in chilly New Hampshire, by the time the race heads south in late February and early March, the surviving candidates are traveling with large entourages of staff, Secret Service agents, and the media. After Robert Kennedy's assassination in 1968, Congress passed a law extending Secret Service protection to major presidential candidates who met certain criteria.

In 1992, none of the candidates requested Secret Service protection early in the process because no one wanted to be associated with the institutions of government at a time when voters were disgusted with Washington. The Secret Service, however, provides excellent logistical support to a presidential campaign, and after New Hampshire the candidates needed all the help they could get to travel to several cities in several different states each day. The Secret Service also helps a candidate look presidential. As the process cuts the number of candidates to a few, voters begin to look harder at these candidates and try to imagine each in the Oval Office, the president's office at the White House. The Secret Service also helps the campaign pay for the chartered jet it needs to campaign across a larger geographic area after the New Hampshire primary. The U.S. Treasury Department pays the traveling costs of the Secret Service just as each media organization reimburses the campaign for the costs of its reporters and crews.

The hottest candidates attract the largest press corps and the most television coverage. By the end of the general election campaign in late October, the leading presidential campaigns travel with two or more jets. The second press charter where the extra television crews and correspondents for smaller news organizations ride is called the zoo plane. According to campaign legend, the zoo plane got its name because television technicians had a tendency to behave like the denizens of a fraternity animal house.

Buchanan's "Guerrilla" Style Campaign

New Hampshire would represent the peak of the Buchanan campaign because the Buchanan crusade with its young and inexperienced staff was no match for the power of an incumbent president. In the heady days after the New Hampshire primary anything seemed possible. Buchanan went home to northern Virginia on Wednesday, February 19, the day after the New Hampshire primary, to regroup, do his laundry, and repack his bags. He flew from suburban Washington to Augusta, Georgia, on Friday, February 21 to take his campaign south. Unlike President Bush who cannot travel anywhere without several days notice because of security considerations, Buchanan ran a lightweight, low to the ground, guerrilla campaign. The first day showed the flexibility of a guerrilla effort. He flew first to Augusta, Georgia, to raise the Buchanan flag in the state, the electoral gateway to the Southern primaries. "We're going to give George Bush the battle of his life right here in Georgia," he said to a throng of supporters at the ironically named Bush Field. "Our objective is to expose the differences between two candidates for the Republican nomination. We will expose the fact that with George Bush we thought we had a continuance of Ronald Reagan's policies in Washington. Instead, we got warmed over Jimmy Carter."

Buchanan said it was time to rededicate the Republican party to the principles of lower taxes, less government, and "a foreign policy that puts America first." And in this region where millions of white voters broke with the national Democratic party over racial issues, Buchanan modified the basic campaign pitch that he had polished in New Hampshire to appeal to a different constituency. He added the issue of racial "quotas" to the mix. "I believe all forms of discrimination based on race and gender are wrong," he declared. "I believe that quotas of any kind are wrong and that you do not change the invidious nature of racial quotas simply by changing the color of the beneficiary." If elected president, he said, "all forms of reverse discrimination will be out of the federal government lock, stock, and barrel."

Then the old Convair headed off to Charleston, South Carolina, where Buchanan decided to crash a Republican party event as an uninvited guest. The Southern Republican Leadership Conference refused to allow Buchanan to speak at its meeting even though it had invited Bush. Buchanan flew into town anyway, just minutes before President Bush, to hold a press conference two blocks away from the meeting. "We're going to take this battle to the grassroots until they have no other choice but to debate us face to face," he vowed. He offered a preview of what would be a new emphasis on affirmative action as well as renewed focus on trade policies in this region where textile plants were having difficulty competing with foreign competition. But one incident on the highway into town from the airport showed the stark differences in this David and Goliath battle. The Buchanan motorcade, still a relatively modest affair because the Secret Service had not yet been assigned to him, got stuck in traffic, which had been stopped by the local police to make way for the presidential motorcade.

Buchanan's Georgia Bus Tour

At first, Buchanan seemed to be the captive of his schedulers who thought he needed to make appearances in several different states. The next day in Florida he plaintively complained in public about how he needed to get back to Georgia because it was a make or break state for him. If Buchanan did not do well in Georgia, he could forget about doing better in the contests taking place a week later. Although Bush was more popular in Georgia than in New Hampshire, the Buchanan strategists viewed Georgia as a potentially receptive area for Buchanan's conservative message because of two factors: a more socially conservative environment and a larger number of conservatives, specifically Democratic conservatives. Georgia has no party registration so that voters who consider themselves Democrats could cross over and vote in the Republican primary to send George Bush a message if they chose.

Buchanan aggressively courted the conservative rural Georgians by raising bitterly resented federal court rulings that forced Georgians and other Southerners to treat black residents the same as white. He tried to recapture the magic of New Hampshire with a three-day bus trip through rural Georgia where he delivered a racially-tinged message to all-white crowds aimed at drawing disaffected Democrats to his cause. "We're asking for Republican votes on Tuesday and I'm asking for independent votes on Tuesday and I'm asking for Democrats who are conservatives and traditionalists, as I am, to come across and vote in the Republican primary and give us that kind of victory we had in New Hampshire," he said at the ceremonial opening of his Georgia campaign headquarters in Newnan, a small town 40 minutes south of Atlanta. "It's not simply Republicans but Democrats and independents who are ready for a new American revolution that takes over from both parties in Washington, D.C.," he said at Columbus College in Columbus. "There is only one candidate running against the establishment of both parties," he said in Tifton. "This state is the New Hampshire of the South. New Hampshire shook him up and put him on the canvass. Now they are up but they are a little groggy. Well, Georgia comes on Tuesday and in your hands lies the fate and future of my campaign. These folks in Washington really cannot defend their record of the last three years. We punched a hole in that blimp in

New Hampshire. If we punch another one in it in Georgia, it will come down overnight. If the headlines out of Georgia on Tuesday look like the headlines out of New Hampshire, you can shake up this nation and this world. It can be done.''

On the second day of the bus tour through small towns and cities in southern Georgia, Buchanan accused President Bush of "caving" to congressional pressure on a racial "quota" bill, the Civil Rights Act of 1991, and railed against "reverse discrimination" and federal efforts to force Southern compliance with the landmark civil rights laws of the 1960s. "The quota bill was virtually drafted by Teddy Kennedy," said Buchanan who drew guffaws with a joke about how he had great respect for Kennedy, the senior senator from Massachusetts, because "how many 59-year-old men do you know who still go to Florida for spring break?" This joke was a clear reference to the previous year's Easter weekend visit to Palm Beach that resulted in rape charges being leveled against Kennedy's nephew, William Kennedy Smith. "After saying I'll never sign a quota bill, he (Bush) went ahead and signed it. It puts the burden of proof on businessmen who are accused to prove their innocence and that is not the American way," he said in Griffin. Buchanan ripped into the federal review of Southern state elections mandated by the Voting Rights Act 1965 that made one person, one vote the law of the land by outlawing practices that discriminated against blacks in the South. "Before you could have your primary, your whole state government had to go hat in hand up to George Bush's Justice Department and get some liberal Republican to say whether or not you folks can have a primary and when you can have a primary," he said to a responsive audience from the Houston County Courthouse steps in Perry. "Some sixteen states are under that law. That is an act of regional discrimination against the South."

"I was born and raised in Washington, D.C.," he said stirring an anti-establishment pitch to the mix. "They are not all that smart up there, and they are not better than everybody else in the country. Every single state should be under the same law, every single one of them." In Griffin, he tied together several themes when he denounced "one party government," in Washington. "They conspired together on the tax increase and they conspired together on the quota bill," he said.

Despite only 24-hours notice for the outdoor series of rallies, Buchanan drew enthusiastic crowds of local townspeople who brought their children and hoisted the small ones onto their shoulders to see the presidential candidate. The Secret Service had joined the campaign by this point so the motorcade was more impressive. His bus, newly equipped with a sound system on the roof, roared up to each event blaring march tunes. Willie Nelson's "On the Road Again," acted as the musical punctuation point to end each event and to signal the traveling press to get back on the bus.

Because Georgia falls in the Bible Belt, the rural South where many conservative evangelical Christians live, Buchanan tried to cast Bush as someone who condoned federal support for pornography. His campaign aired a graphic television ad attacking the Bush administration for subsidizing through a National Endowment of the Arts grant a controversial documentary film that featured leather-clad homosexuals. The ad included a clip from the documentary of a group of scantily clad men dancing. The ad was so graphic that it made news and led the Atlanta television newscasts. Buchanan charged that the film represented a deliberate attempt to "injure, wound, offend, and insult Americans of traditional values and Christians and conservatives." To the state legislature he said, "I don't care what they do in their garrets with their precious bodily fluids and their bullwhips. But I tell you if I am president, I will shut down that thing, padlock the door, and fumigate the building." In Columbus, he added, "The artsy-craftsy crowd of the eastern establishment is going to lose its upholstered playpen." These were fighting words to the conservative sensibilities of Georgians who roared with delight every time he said them.

Buchanan was euphoric. As his three-day bus trip wound down, he spoke to a crowd in Lawrenceville about his cause:

We went down in south Georgia today and last night, and I picked up the signs of the same kind of momentum here in Georgia that we saw up in New Hampshire during those final days. I think there is a real chance the history we made in New Hampshire can be repeated here. And if it is repeated here, this campaign can go right on to Mississippi and Louisiana and all the way to that convention in Houston, and we can still make it all the way to the White House. But we need your support here in Georgia. The president is down here now. They sent down Danny Boy the other day. That didn't quite do it so now he is down here himself. They are nervous there in the White House. You know, they ought to be nervous, and the reason they are nervous is because we are down here and we are telling the truth about their record. And we are telling the truth about what they said they would do and about what they did. When they talked about not raising taxes and then raised taxes. They talked about never signing a quota bill and then they signed a quota bill. That is why I got into this race because I wasn't going to let the 1992 campaign go by without conservatism and traditionalism having at least one voice and one champion in the great debate of 1992.

Not even the pollsters would guess at how many conservative white Democrats might cross over to vote for Buchanan in the Republican primary in Georgia on March 3, but it was possible that the crossover vote would be considerable and that put a strong showing for Buchanan within reach. Buchanan attracted enthusiastic crowds in 18 different rural Georgia towns during his bus trip. At this point, Buchanan and his strategists thought it was possible to beat Bush through a prolonged siege. "Bush will not be killed by a single blow. He will be killed by a thousand cuts," said Paul Erickson, a brilliant young lawyer and movie maker who was the national political director for Buchanan's campaign. Erickson said that Buchanan might be able to win the nomination if he continued to do well in the primaries. If not, then Buchanan might be able to expose Bush as too weak to win a general election. In that case, the nomination might be wrested away during a floor fight at the Republican National Convention in Houston.

Bush's Reaction to Buchanan

Such strategy was not without foundation. The Bush-Quayle reelection campaign was reacting to everything Buchanan said and did. After insisting for months that the nation's economy was doing fine, Bush conceded that the nation was in a recession. Bush admitted that he made a mistake when he agreed to raise taxes in an interview with the *Atlanta Constitution*. He fired the head of the National Endowment of the Arts. He delayed action on a foreign aid bill. These actions led Buchanan to crow that he might not be winning the election, but he was driving and winning the national debate.

The Results of Georgia, Colorado, and Maryland Primaries

Moreover, Buchanan was attracting so much attention that his campaign had to replace the rickety Convair with an equally ancient DC 9 to accommodate the larger press corps that included network television crews. "They are very, very nervous," Buchanan said of the Bush White House. Buchanan failed to deliver a knockout punch in Georgia where he pulled 36 percent of the vote, but he did well enough to stay in the race because it was clear that Bush had troubles. Colorado and Maryland held Republican primary contests on the same day as Georgia. Although Buchanan did not so much as set his foot in either state, he pulled 30 percent of the vote in each state.

If the election results were exposing the soft underbelly of Bush's candidacy, then they also suggested limitations to Buchanan's own candidacy. The first contests were beginning to show that Buchanan was bumping against a natural ceiling of his own appeal in a Republican primary. Buchanan was already conceding that he could not win the nomination by running second all the time. "You cannot win the silver medal 50 times in a two man race and expect to be nominated," he said. His supporters worried about the daunting difference in resources between the two campaigns. "There is never enough time and money," said Frank Luntz, the campaign's 30-year-old pollster.

SUPER TUESDAY

With pressure mounting for Buchanan to grab the gold from George Bush by beating him someplace somewhere soon, the drive to Super Tuesday, then a week away, became a frantic campaign to "do media" and reach as many media markets as possible by jet and satellite. In the six days between the Georgia primary and the 11 state contests on March 10, Buchanan could not hope to shake enough hands or meet enough people, so, like the other presidential candidates, he reached out to voters through their living room television sets and on their car radios. The day after the Georgia primary on March 4, Buchanan granted 17 "exclusive" radio and television interviews, many in key Southern states. By 6:50 a.m., after about three and a half hours sleep, he had finished six television interviews, three on national network television, and two on radio.

A Day in the Life . . . of a Presidential Candidate

Buchanan's telephone at the Holiday Inn in Shreveport, Louisiana, rang at about 4:30 a.m. to wake him up. The campaign had flown from Atlanta to Shreveport late the night before after a giddy election night rally. His schedule called for him to be at a hotel meeting room 30 minutes later so that a local make-up artist, Debra David, could apply his television make-up for several TV appearances. At 5:30 a.m. he taped a segment for "Good Morning America" on ABC. At 6:10 a.m. he appeared live on the "Today Show" on NBC. Bryant Gumbel, the co-host of the "Today Show," asked Buchanan, a devout Roman Catholic, what he intended to give up for Lent because it was Ash Wednesday, the first day of Lent. "Losing," shot back Buchanan. At 6:40 a.m. a campaign aide drove him to a local television station KSLA for a live 7 a.m. appearance on CNN.

Meanwhile, the traveling press corps struggled down to the lobby with their luggage and gear to make the 7:30 a.m. baggage call and grab a quick breakfast before Buchanan's return to the hotel to speak to supporters who were crowded into the ballroom. (The luggage and equipment must be swept for bombs and explosives and packed onto the airplane in advance.) "Last night our campaign really came of age," he said after being introduced as "a true American patriot" by a local supporter. "We've only been alive as a national campaign for 12 weeks, now we are shaking up the nation and shaking up the world." Then in a concession to realism, Buchanan said, "The legs are a little rubbery. But he still outweighs me by 100 pounds."

Buchanan then moved into the deserted hotel cocktail lounge to hold his first press conference of the day. He conceded that Bush had command of the resources needed to capture the delegates for the Republican nomination but he also sounded a warning. The nomination would be a Pyrrhic or empty victory if Bush failed to articulate a vision for the future and win the support of those key voters who determine the outcome of national elections. "I think

President Bush should begin to give consideration to standing (sic) down as a candidate for renomination for the Republican party for president of the United States," he said at the press conference. "Mr. Bush is in danger of becoming the Jimmy Carter of the Republican party." The campaign then loaded up the buses for a drive to Mansfield Street to tour an A T & T facility at 9:30 a.m. Buchanan did not make any news there, but he was photographed talking to workers and that picture would be relayed to hundreds of thousands of Louisiana voters on local television. Then the entourage drove to the Shreveport Regional Airport to fly to Baton Rouge, an hour away. In Baton Route, he delivered a luncheon speech at the Sheraton Hotel and then held another press conference. "Why is he running for a second term? What does he want to do? Where does he want to take the country? For the life of me, I don't know what George Bush really believes. ... He is winning the primaries but losing the debate," he said. "But I am winning (the debate) by default because they are not engaged."

"Don't let the Bush people tell you he is the only electable candidate," cautioned Buchanan at the lunch. "He is an endangered species if he is at the top of our ticket." Frank Luntz analyzed the election day exit poll results for Buchanan. (Exit polls are surveys of voters conducted as they leave the polls and are considered extremely reliable barometers of voter opinion.) He told Buchanan that Bush won the hard-core Republican vote but lost the Reagan Democrats, independents, young people, and other key swing constituencies. Luntz said Bush's political base was contracting and Bush risked losing the swing voters just as Jimmy Carter had lost them to Ronald Reagan in 1980. "And he is losing to a candidate who twelve weeks ago was a television commentator," said Buchanan, a first time candidate for public office who made his living as a syndicated columnist and TV commentator until announcing his candidacy December 10. "Mr. Bush is losing the votes which are vital to the Republican party not only to maintain the White House but to maintain strength we have in the House and Senate. It is arguable that Pat Buchanan would be a stronger candidate in a general election," he said.

The daily schedule called for Buchanan to speak to students at the Baton Rouge Magnet School at 2 p.m., but the question and answer session was canceled. No time. His charter flight flew to Lafayette where he held another press conference and spoke to supporters at a Hilton Hotel reception."This is good, conservative country," said Buchanan. "There is only one authentic conservative left in the race, and he is in Lafayette tonight." The entire entourage then drove to the Acadia Village in Vermillionville where he spoke at a Cajun Fais-do-do festival at 6 p.m. Afterwards, the charter flight held on the tarmac for a few extra minutes so that local police could deliver a reporter who missed the press bus. Steve Lansing, a local police officer, sped the embarrassed journalist to the airport in a cruiser with a great show of flashing lights and screaming sirens. As a joke, the Secret Service agents marched the reporter onto the plane in handcuffs. The joke was welcome at this exhausting point in a long day, and Buchanan howled with laughter. Late that night, the campaign made one extra stop at the Tulsa, Oklahoma, airport so he could hold his fourth press conference of the day and grant live one-on-one interviews for local evening newscasts. The day ended near midnight in Oklahoma City. This 20-hour day was a typical Super Tuesday campaign day for a presidential candidate in 1992.

Buchanan's Television Experience

Buchanan's strength as a candidate rested in his skill as a television performer and master of the succinct sound bite. After spending almost a decade in a television studio as the co-host of a daily, television show "Crossfire" for Cable News Network and appearing as a regular guest on other public affairs television shows, Buchanan had a command and ease with television unusual for a political candidate even in media-conscious times. His media skills showed how an articulate candidate with something to say could challenge a sitting president of the United States and be taken seriously.

One day in Florida, Buchanan showed up for what he thought was a 15-minute live interview on a Florida television station only to be informed that the station was breaking into regular programming to let him speak directly into the camera for 15 minutes. He did it without notice or notes. "The only way to get his message out is to go directly to the people. The only way to do that is through the media," said press secretary Greg Mueller who described himself as a "media hustler." Mueller offered "exclusive" interviews with Buchanan to every major radio station and television station in each market to which the campaign traveled. Local stations eager to talk to a presidential candidate never turned him down.

Buchanan's 30 years as a newspaper editorialist, presidential speech writer, and syndicated columnist also gave him an intuitive understanding of the workings of the electronic and print media that was more characteristic of a media professional than a politician. Indeed, he had earned a master's degree in journalism from the Columbia School of Journalism and regarded himself as a journalist rather than a politician. Reporters enjoyed covering him because he delivered crisp, timely, and newsworthy quotes seemingly effortlessly and repeated them with a discipline that made it clear why he had been director of communications for the Great Communicator himself, Ronald Reagan. For his part, Buchanan liked and respected the press. He wore three wireless microphones (and ruined countless expensive Hermes silk ties) while campaigning so that the three network television crews covering his campaign could capture every word he spoke as he walked to and from events and not have to rely upon boom mikes held over his head. Many candidates would not be trusted by their handlers to wear the mikes for fear they might misspeak. Just before delivering his speeches, Buchanan used to routinely whip open his suit jacket and flick on the switches hooked onto his belt to open the microphones.

The Buchanan campaign estimated that it attracted about twice the amount of free media time, that is news interviews on local and national radio and television stations, as it had paid for in electronic advertising. They rarely passed up an opportunity to maximize the media exposure. While driving to appearances from the airport, Buchanan would call local radio stations from a cellular telephone in his car. The Bush and Buchanan campaigns tried to make in-person appearances in the same media markets at the same time, but satellite technology gave Buchanan the opportunity to be where President Bush was even while campaigning in a different state. After a Buchanan campaign official noticed HUD Secretary Jack Kemp, a top Bush surrogate, appearing via satellite on a number of Southern television stations, the campaign arranged to purchase its own satellite time in Dallas for interviews that were then offered to local television stations across the South. "If I had my way," said Mueller who runs his own public relations firm in Washington, "I'd have Pat campaign from a couch, put his feet up to do radio and then spin around, put on his tie and do live TV feeds."

CONCLUSION

Buchanan demonstrated the importance of a clear and articulate message in a political campaign, and his style and media savvy underscored the importance of conveying that message to masses of voters through the media. The candidates who left behind the deepest footprints on the campaign trail in 1992 were those who were most innovative and aggressive in their use of the media to communicate with voters. The traditional dominant role of the press had been changing over the years as candidates developed alternative ways of reaching the people. In 1992, it was necessary for the press to monitor television and radio broadcasts to keep informed of the campaign developments.

Buchanan acted out the classic "spoiler" role in the Republican contest because his candidacy exposed deep divisions within the Republican party as well as serious weaknesses in President Bush's political standing with the party faithful, particularly the conservatives. Like most spoilers, Buchanan softened up Bush for the Democratic kill in the fall. The Republicans who backed Buchanan had a hard time becoming enthusiastic about Bush, and many never could muster much excitement for the man who beat their favorite. Buchanan, like the unsuccessful Democratic candidates, helped to educate the voters, changed the dynamic of the campaign, highlighted issues that otherwise might have been ignored, and raised the stakes for victory.

Chapter 6

Piercing the Press Filter: Candidates Try to Reach Voters Directly

THE ROLE OF THE MEDIA AS WATCHDOG

Before the advent of television and talk radio, most voters learned about presidential candidates, their backgrounds, and their positions on the issues from newspaper reports. Today, the public can cull a variety of sources of information on the presidential campaign ranging from computer networks like Prodigy to C-Span, the public access channel that shows real slice-of-life video from the campaign without any commentary. Nevertheless, the national press corps, which includes both electronic and print journalists, still acts as a kind of traffic cop that signals the public and directs attention to major issues and developments.

In some foreign nations, the press is neither free nor independent because it is owned by the government so the newspapers and television newscasts never report anything unfavorable about politicians or the government. In the United States, the media enjoys the protection of the U.S. Constitution. The first Amendment of the Bill of Rights says: "Congress shall make no law respecting an establishment of religion, or prohibiting the free exercise thereof; or abridging the freedom of speech, or of the press; or the right of the people peaceably to assemble, and to petition the Government for a redress of grievances."

This right carries with it major responsibilities to dig out the true facts and present to the readers and viewers as accurate a view of reality as is possible. This task is not always easy, and individual news organizations and reporters can and do make mistakes. Commercial and competitive pressure also conspire at times to make it difficult for the media to do its job properly. Except for public broadcasting, which is subsidized by the government, all of the major news organizations in the United States, including every major newspaper and every television network, are privately owned businesses. These commercial enterprises must make more money than they spend or go out of business. They make money by selling advertisements. They spend money on everything from news anchor's salaries to ink. The major news organizations build a figurative fire wall between news and advertising sections so that the news reporters can do their jobs without any interference from the businesses that purchase ads in the paper or buy commercial time during the news broadcasts. Smaller news organizations with less resources and smaller staffs sometimes have a harder time resisting the pressure of advertisers or powerful community interests to kill a story that puts those interests in a bad light.

THE TABLOIDS IN THE 1992 CAMPAIGN

No news organization likes to miss a big story or be beaten by its competition on a major breaking story. The fierce fight to get the story first can put pressure on a news organization to bend its own rules and standards. Not every publication or broadcast outlet takes its responsibilities to the public seriously. Even major news organizations sometimes feel torn between a sensational story that will sell newspapers and a sober story that is less titillating but more responsible. But there is a growing business, an illegitimate press, that makes no effort to present the facts in a cold, dispassionate, and accurate light. The tabloid supermarket press, shock radio, and tabloid television traffic in scandal, sensationalism, and gossip. They rarely let the facts stand in the way of a hot story. In 1992, much to the dismay of the legitimate press, the tabloid press played a major role in unleashing the first major controversy of the campaign.

Reporting of Gossip and Rumor: Dukakis in 1988

Even before he announced his candidacy, Bill Clinton and his wife Hillary had breakfast with a group of reporters in Washington and admitted that their marriage had hit some rough patches but that they had worked things out. They also said that they considered any history of trouble in their marriage their private business and intended to say nothing more about it. This position sounded fine to most national political reporters. No serious reporter is comfortable about digging through the garbage of public figures for gossip. While any serious analysis of a would-be president's character includes an examination of past conduct in both private and public, there is also a commonsense rule that extends some limited bit of privacy to public figures. In the past two presidential campaigns, this "privacy" rule had been flaunted and broken, and neither the politicians nor the press felt very comfortable about it. In fact, the "rules" are very loose ones. Reporters, editors, and producers generally must make a subjective judgment about information that the public needs to know, and those judgments can vary depending upon the circumstances and personalities involved.

In 1992, the national press felt particularly leery about repeating unfounded gossip or doing stories about personal matters that had no relationship with a candidate's ability to govern. In 1988, a persistent rumor contended that Michael S. Dukakis, the Democratic presidential nominee, had suffered from mental depression and received shock treatments in the late 1970s. This rumor turned out to be false and totally unfounded. It had been started and spread in Massachusetts by his political enemies. When he became a presidential candidate, some supporters of the extremist cult leader Lyndon LaRouche reprinted the rumors with some fictitious elaboration in brochures and distributed them all over the country. Delegates to the Democratic National Convention found the brochures slipped under their hotel room doors in Atlanta in July. Although there was no truth to this rumor, there is something in human nature that likes to gossip. So like many rumors, it was repeated so often that eventually a reporter from the *Boston Herald* asked Dukakis if it was true. Dukakis shrugged off the question as a stupid one unworthy of comment and said nothing. This exchange was reported in the *Boston Globe* the next day. The *Globe* account, carried at the bottom of a daily story about Dukakis, put the rumor into the public domain. Up until that point, the story had been nothing more than a persistent rumor. But the publication of the rumor made it fair game for other news organizations to repeat it by attributing the *Globe* as the source.

The rumor soon acquired a life of its own. During a photo opportunity at the White House, a reporter for a Lyndon LaRouche publication asked President Ronald Reagan about the rumors. Reagan made a bad joke. He said, "Look, I'm not going to pick on an invalid." Although Reagan apologized for his wisecrack later in the day, his offhand comment gave the news media an excuse to do a full-blown story on the mental depression rumors. Dukakis was put in the awkward position of denying the rumors and asserting that he was mentally balanced at a time when many voters had growing reservations about his candidacy because of months of relentless criticism from his opponent George Bush. Dukakis dropped nine percentage points in the public opinion polls that week.

CLINTON AND THE TABLOIDS

The press felt guilty about its role in spreading this unfounded rumor, and in 1992 reporters vowed to do better. But the uncharted territory of junk journalism frustrated those good intentions before the first month of the year had passed. The Clinton campaign was vigilant about rumors about the governor's past conduct involving women and had successfully squelched one rumor in the fall of 1991. A rock groupie named Connie Hamzy from Arkansas sold Penthouse magazine a story in which she claimed that she had a sexual encounter with Clinton at a Little Rock motel. A young Clinton press aide with carrot colored hair named Steve Cohen heard a Little Rock radio talk show host talking about the story and alerted George Stephanopoulos, a deputy campaign manager. Stephanopoulos immediately collected affidavits from witnesses who said that Hamzy had approached Clinton and he had turned her down. He used those affidavits to kill the story, which was mentioned once on CNN Headline News. The next day while celebrating this victory over pizza, Cohen was nicknamed "Scoop." Scoop Cohen now works in the White House press office.

Damage Control

But Clinton was not out of the woods yet. In January, *The Star*, a supermarket tabloid, printed a story that rehashed allegations that Clinton had affairs with several women including Gennifer Flowers. The allegations had been made in a lawsuit filed several years earlier by a disgruntled former state employee who had been fired for using state telephones to make long distance telephone calls to help the Nicaraguan Contras. He later admitted that he made up the charges. When reporters asked Clinton about this story, he said it was an old and false story, and he dismissed *The Star* as a newspaper "that says Martians walk on the earth and cows have human heads." That story was not repeated in the legitimate press because it was so obviously filled with holes.

But *The Star* was not finished with Clinton yet. The publication printed a lurid first-person account from Flowers in a later edition that unleashed a firestorm. The legitimate press wanted nothing to do with this story. *The Star* had paid the woman for her story. Gennifer Flowers, a low-level state employee in Arkansas who had worked in the past as a television news reporter and cabaret singer, claimed she had had a 12-year affair with Bill Clinton. Not only had she been paid for her story, which raised a serious question about whether she was telling the truth or making up the story to get money, but a year before, she also had denied the allegations through her lawyer and flatly stated that she had no relationship with Clinton.

This story would not die, and it began to creep into the legitimate newspapers because local television stations reported the exchanges between reporters traveling with the Clinton campaign and the candidate. At first, the major newspapers stuck the story inside the paper. Within days, however, it had become front page news. Once an allegation like that gets into the public domain, there is a responsibility on the part of the legitimate press to put the matter in context and get to the bottom of it if possible. Responsible reporters worried that they were just passing on gossip. The ethics of this story were debated heatedly in news rooms across the nation. Reporters and editors alike were troubled by it. It ended up getting published and aired because it literally could not be contained, largelybecause of competitive reasons and because it was having a major impact on the presidential race. The Clinton campaign eventually got some control over this story when Clinton and his wife appeared on "60 Minutes" on CBS.

THE IDEAL ROLE OF THE PRESS

The Gennifer Flowers episode soured many voters on the press and encouraged them to look for ways to get the news about the candidates without it first going through the media filter. A candidate typically delivers his or her stump speech several times a day, day after day, week after week, month after month, with little change. For the members of the press corps who travel with the candidate or cover the campaign all the time, this repetition can get pretty tedious. While the speech is new for the audience that hears it each time, it is very, very familiar to the traveling press corps. As a result, reporters look for other stories. This arrangement can be both good and bad. The traveling press acquires so much knowledge and information about a candidacy, that it can produce stories rich in perspective, history, and detail which convey to readers and viewers a clear sense of the candidate and the candidate's positions on issues. If a candidate abruptly changes a position on an issue, the press can alert the public that this candidate has changed. If a candidate says one thing in Claremont, New Hampshire, and just the opposite in Greenville, South Carolina, the press can again flag that discrepancy for the public. But a restless or bored reporter can also focus too much attention on tiny little developments and tactics and become so immersed in how a message is being delivered that the reporter neglects to tell readers and viewers what the message is.

How Politicians Attempt to Control the Press

It is in the interests of politicians to present an idealized public image of themselves that is unmarred by the inevitable facts and foibles that make everyone human. The press corps helps to put this gauzy public image into perspective with a reality check. During political campaigns there is an endless struggle between the candidate and his staff and the press corps over access to the candidate and over the issues of the moment. During the month of June when Perot's grassroots army was multiplying across the land and Perot was becoming a significant force in the presidential campaign, the press corps wanted Clinton to talk about Perot. It was not in Clinton's interest to answer questions about an opponent, so the Clinton campaign sharply restricted access to Clinton, even for his traveling press corps, to minimize the opportunity for the press to even question him about Perot. In that way, the press corps was almost forced to report on what Clinton was saying at public appearances. This arrangement was better for Clinton because he was trying to repair his public image and look like a man of substance. Throughout the Reagan and Bush presidencies, the press corps' ability to question the president in person had been sharply curtailed. The public relations specialists who worked for Reagan were masterful political salesmen who felt the press only complicated their job so they cut out the press.

In 1992, Ross Perot carried this isolation from the press to an extreme. He rarely dealt directly with the press corps. When he

The turning point for Bill Clinton's campaign took place in June when he used television talk shows and town meetings to reshape his public image. Bryant Gumbel of the "Today Show" hosted an extraordinary one-hour session with Clinton. (Photo courtesy of National Broadcasting Company.)

finally decided to run for president on October 1, he campaigned almost exclusively for 33 days through paid advertising and on the three televised presidential debates. He made only a handful of public appearances and took questions from the press corps infrequently. A stand-in, Orson Swindle, a former prisoner of war who headed up Perot's grassroots organization, held daily press briefings at the Dallas headquarters for much of the month, but he often had no idea what Perot was thinking or doing.

CLINTON'S CHANGING NEED FOR THE PRESS

At the beginning of the nominating season, all of the challengers were eager to talk to the press because they needed to publicize their ideas and their candidacies. As Clinton moved closer to clinching his party's nomination, his need changed. He no longer needed publicity at almost any cost; he needed the right type of publicity about the right types of issues. By the time the nominating season ended in June, many Americans considered him a draft-dodging ladies' man rather than a prospective president. His public image had become a cartoon caricature of a candidate. Even Clinton could no longer recognize himself. He complained to Craig Smith, his longtime political aide from Arkansas, "I get up every morning and read these stories in the paper and say 'Who is this guy?' It's not me."

Bill Clinton won the Democratic Party nomination but emerged from the primaries battered and scarred. (Cartoon by Dan Wasserman, *Boston Globe*, distributed by LA Times Syndicate.)

Improving Clinton's Image on the Talk Show Circuit

His challenge in June when he had fallen into third place in the polls behind Perot and Bush was to reassemble a more compelling public image and shift the campaign back to his ideas for doing right by the middle class people who worked hard and played by the rules. To execute this strategy, press access to him became more restricted. He launched an aggressive campaign in June to sidestep the regular press and revive his candidacy through television appearances that helped to dispel lingering questions about his character. The first appearance came the day after the California primary on June 3 on the "Arsenio Hall Show." When the show opened that night, the regular band, The Posse, had a new sax player, a big guy from Arkansas named Bill Clinton. Clinton borrowed a pair of dark sunglasses from Paul Begala, the young political consultant who traveled with him, and tooted away on the song, "Heartbreak Hotel," one of the hits of his all-time favorite rock and roll singer, Elvis Presley. He looked very cool.

This appearance shocked the political pundits in Washington. They thought such behavior undignified for a prospective president. But the public apparently did not share that view. Arsenio Hall's young audience not only enjoyed Clinton playing his saxophone but got to listen to Clinton discuss with Hall serious issues like civil rights. The television audience that night saw several sides of a multifaceted man. The very next night, back in Little Rock, Clinton appeared on "Larry King Live," the CNN show that launched the Perot candidacy, from the governor's mansion.

Clinton's campaign staff pleaded for invitations and accepted appearances on virtually every network television show that would allow him to talk at some length about issues with either an interviewer or an audience of voters. Mandy Grunwald, a media consultant to Clinton, was the principle architect of this strategy. This young woman avidly read *People* magazine every week and regularly video-surfed with her television zapper. She understood popular culture and instinctively knew that network news shows were no longer the primary source of information on presidential candidates. The Freedom Forum Media Studies Center at Columbia University found that Clinton appeared 47 times on five popular talk shows in 1992, Ross Perot appeared 33 times, and Bush (who got into the talk show game late) only 16 times.

The following week, Clinton flew to New York to appear on the "Today Show" for a full hour, one half of the entire show. The morning news shows typically limit each topic to six minutes. Nine minutes is endless on morning television. A full 60 minutes was unheard of before this appearance. The show's co-host Bryant Gumbel deliberately stayed low key and deferred to the viewers to question the candidate by telephone. Clinton answered questions on topics ranging from the nuclear test ban treaty to New York's Shock Jock, Howard Stern. The next week, a competing show, "Good Morning America," on ABC one-upped NBC by giving Clinton two full hours, the entire television show. "CBS This Morning" got into the act pretty quickly and devoted the show to Clinton on Monday, June 15. He flew from New York to California so he could appear the next day on a special 90-minute broadcast on MTV, the first 24-hour video music network.

Reaching the MTV Audience

The typical MTV viewing audience of 15 million young Americans made up about half of all 18 to 24 year olds in the

Diane Sawyer of ABC's "Prime Time Live" interviewed Bill and Hillary Clinton. (Photo courtesy of Capital Cities/ABC Inc.)

country. This age group has the poorest voting record. As citizens age, they tend to become more involved in politics and more interested in voting because as homeowners and taxpayers and parents they have a more direct interest in the workings of government. The level of taxation and quality of public schools are issues that often prod political interest in people as they age. Young people tend to be distracted by other things even though it is their future that is at stake. MTV ran an aggressive educational campaign called "Choose or Lose" in 1992 in an attempt to demystify the political process for young adults.

Tabitha Soren, the 24-year-old campaign reporter for MTV, prepared reports on various aspects of the campaign that were broadcast with the flash and dash of a rock video complete with terrific music in the background. The reports had featured Pat Buchanan and the Democratic challengers, but the Clinton session in Hollywood was different because Clinton would be answering the questions of young people whom MTV scouts found at local universities and businesses. "The key thing here is to make the young people the king of the show," explained Tom Freston, the chairman and CEO of MTV Networks, before the taping began. The program was originally scheduled to last for an hour, but the producers extended it for another half hour so more members of the audience could ask Clinton questions.

He spoke about everything from his astrological sign (Leo: his birthday is Aug. 19) to what it was like to have a strong, independent woman as a wife. He was asked what affect growing up in an alcoholic household had on him. (His stepfather Roger Clinton had been an alcoholic who beat Bill Clinton's mother when he was drunk. When Bill Clinton was barely in his teens, he stood up to his stepfather to protect his mother, Virginia.) The question came from a 20-year-old economics student, and Clinton gave a thoughtful answer. Clinton explained that his half-brother Roger Clinton, Jr., had developed a serious drug problem and been arrested some years earlier. The entire family went into family therapy to help Roger, Jr., and Bill Clinton had thought a lot about what it was like to be an adult child of an alcoholic during those sessions. He told the student that the experience had left him with good and bad characteristics. "The good thing is I'm always trying to make things better," he said. "The bad thing is when I try so hard to make peace when you have to just cut it and recognize that conflict is inevitable." One student impishly asked him that if he had to do it again and try marijuana for the first time, would he inhale? In New York earlier in the spring, Clinton had confessed that he had tried marijuana once as a student at Oxford, but being asthmatic, he had not inhaled. The answer opened him to much ridicule from his peers. Clinton grinned and said that given another chance he would inhale this time.

The MTV show was broadcast at least six times over the next few days. Two days later on Thursday, Clinton appeared again on "Larry King Live," and the next day he granted interviews to local television stations by satellite from a studio in Little Rock. On Sunday, he flew to Atlanta to take questions from local voters at a town meeting set up by a local Atlanta television station. A week earlier, the Democratic National Committee had given him the money to buy a half hour of prime network time to broadcast a town meeting from Pittsburgh. This exhaustive television campaign helped Clinton to give the public a better sense of what he was like as a person and talk about his proposals for the nation.

SPECIAL INTEREST GROUPS

At the same time that Clinton was reintroducing himself to the public through the television shows, he was also trying to show voters that he was not beholden to the interests and constituency groups that favor the Democratic party. "Special interest" has become a shorthand expression in politics to cover virtually any organized interest from utility industry executives to members of the United Auto Workers. During any political campaign, organizations that represent a particular point of view or group of people in the same profession will lobby candidates to champion their cause, support those who agree with them, and work against those who disagree with them. These groups represent democracy in action.

During the 1992 campaign, the groups that supported abortion rights and groups that wanted to outlaw abortion, were active in backing the Democratic and Republican candidates who reflected their views. Gun owners who opposed any restrictions on a citizen's right to purchase and own firearms were wooed by Patrick J. Buchanan in New Hampshire. Clinton and Tsongas duked it out to win the enormous senior citizen vote in Florida, the home of millions of retired people. Clinton accused Tsongas of being against the automatic cost of living increase given each year to Social Security recipients. Tsongas angrily accused Clinton of distorting his position but lacked the money and organization to get that message out. In Michigan, the heart of the auto industry in the United States, Jerry Brown wore a United Auto Workers jacket as he campaigned and accused Clinton of being against workers because of his support for free trade. The influence of the auto workers in this Rustbelt state was so great that their concerns spilled into the Republican primary where Pat Buchanan was making a final valiant attempt to recover the momentum he had in New Hampshire. Buchanan aired a tough television ad that noted that the top officials in the Bush campaign were registered foreign

After NBC's Katie Couric interviewed Ross Perot on the "Today Show," he complained that she was too tough on him and, like other female journalists at the network, "trying to prove her manhood." (Photo courtesy of National Broadcasting Company.)

agents, or lobbyists, in Washington for foreign interests including the Japanese auto makers who were producing the cars that put the Michigan auto workers out of work. But Bush countered with an ad that highlighted the fact that Buchanan drove a foreign car himself, a fancy Mercedes Benz. The car really belonged to Buchanan's wife Shelley but the political point was well taken in Michigan where auto workers jeered at Buchanan and told him to go home.

Democrats and Special Interest Groups

When the term "special interest" was first introduced in modern politics, it generally referred to big business and moneyed interests. The Democrats accused the Republicans of being beholden to those "special interests" who traditionally financed Republican campaigns, the wealthy corporate captains of American industry. But the Republicans turned the tables on the Democrats during the Reagan administration and stuck the label onto traditional Democratic party constituencies including African Americans and other minority group members, feminists, and labor union members—groups that rank among the most loyal Democrats. This strategy was effectively used to discredit the 1984 Democratic party nominee, Walter F. Mondale, a liberal Democrat who was responsive to these constituencies and selected the first woman to run on a major party ticket as the vice presidential candidate that year, a congresswoman from Queens named Geraldine Ferraro. Mondale lost the election in a landslide to Ronald Reagan. While few observers thought that any Democrat would have been able to beat Reagan that year, the Republicans effectively questioned Mondale's independence and painted him as a captive of the Democratic party's "special interests."

This tactic was so successful that a group of moderate Southern Democrats, including Bill Clinton, the governor of Arkansas, established the Democratic Leadership Council (DLC) in an attempt to steer the national party away from special interest politics and towards a more mainstream and independent route to improve the Democrats' chances of winning a presidential election. This group included many of the same politicians who dreamed up Super Tuesday primary day, the mostly Southern primary contests designed to help a more moderate presidential candidate.

CLINTON'S MIDDLE-OF-THE-ROAD STRATEGY

As a founding member of the DLC, Clinton was sensitive to the Republican charges against national Democratic leaders. During those critical weeks in June, he took a number of steps to show his independence. Although this period of time following the nominating season and before the Democratic National Convention is typically used to consolidate the party base voters into a rock solid core, Clinton instead seemed to be doing everything he could to alienate these bedrock constituents. He gambled that it was more important to show the nonpartisan independent voters who make the difference in November that he was independent enough to put the public interest ahead of the special interest. Because the Democratic party core constituency groups could not support a Republican who was totally at odds with their policies, it was a safe bet for Clinton that most of these good Democrats would stick with him because they had no place else to go.

The strategy began to unfold on Saturday, June 13 in Washington. On Saturday morning, he told a group of big city mayors that he could not embrace their very expensive proposal to send $35.8 billion in federal money to the mayors for local construction projects. These mayors and their constituents, the people who live in places like Atlanta, East Orange, Boston, and Chicago, are staunch Democratic voters. Clinton later came out with a plan that included some aspects of the mayors' proposal. Because they are practical politicians, they were happy with half a loaf. On Saturday afternoon, he delivered a speech to the Rainbow Coalition, a multiracial group established by Reverend Jesse L. Jackson. The speech started out as a crowd pleaser. He said things like, "I am tired of people with trust funds telling people on food stamps how to live." He criticized the Republican administrations for being insensitive to poor people and members of minority groups. But then he dropped a bomb when he singled out for criticism the racist statements made by Sister Souljah, a young black rap artist.

During an interview with the *Washington Post* some months earlier, Sister Souljah had suggested that if black people could kill other black people during the rioting in Los Angeles which followed the not-guilty verdict against the white police officers accused of beating a black motorist, then why couldn't they kill white people, too? She also said that she had never met a good white person. Clinton said that such racist remarks were wrong whether they came from a black or a white person. In fact, he said she sounded like David Duke, the former Ku Klux Klan leader and white supremacist.

Jesse Jackson, a two-time candidate for president himself and a major leader of the African-American community, sat stony faced during the speech. For the next week, Jackson wavered between anger and appeasement. On the one hand, he was furious because he thought that Clinton was criticizing a black person in order to curry the favor of the conservative white Southern voters who had abandoned Democratic nominees in presidential elections for more than 20 years. On the other hand, he understood that Clinton had criticized many different groups for racial intolerance including conservative Jews in New York and the conservative white ethnic voters of Macomb County in Michigan. As the controversy raged on, Clinton stuck to his guns. Standing on the tarmac at the airport in New York the next day, Clinton told the reporters who traveled with him that "A president should draw a clear line of distinction between what is right and what is not right. To say that some people ought to be killed instead of others or that there were no good people of a certain race, that is just not right and we can't have it."

Two days later, Clinton flew to California to speak at the United Auto Workers union convention. The auto workers were among the labor union groups most opposed to a trade treaty being negotiated by the United States with Mexico and Canada. This North American Free Trade Agreement would turn all of North America into one big market and remove trade barriers so that manufacturers in Mexico could sell products easily in the United States and Canada and vice versa. The UAW feared that this trade agreement could cost their members jobs because it was far cheaper to manufacture products in Mexico where wages and environmental standards are lower than those in the United States. Clinton was basically a free trader and believed that the fewer barriers to trade—barriers like import fees or taxes on products made overseas—the better. He also understood the fears of the unions that represented the interests of average working people who stood to lose their jobs, but he warned these auto workers to face up to the reality that they were going to lose jobs whether there was a treaty or not. Hundreds of thousands of manufacturing jobs had been leaving the United States for low wage foreign countries for years. His not-so-subtle point was that they better get realistic and look at this trade issue from a broader perspective. A bigger North American market for U.S. products would benefit everyone including the auto workers he argued. The auto workers were not thrilled by his words, but the wider audience reached through the traveling press corps got the message loud and clear: no one owned this Democrat.

On the day of the Sister Souljah incident, Jesse Jackson's daughter Santita serenaded Clinton with a special song titled "Everything Must Change." This Democratic candidate was well on his way to capitalizing on the public's desire for a change in the country.

Chapter 7

Conventioneering: Republican and Democratic National Conventions

On the first night of the Republican National Convention on Monday August, 17, 1992, Ted Maravelias, a 23-year-old ex-football player from Danvers, Massachusetts, sat in the midst of a cheering throng on the floor of the Astrodome in Houston and felt his conservative heart break. He was upset because his political heroes, Ronald Reagan and Patrick J. Buchanan, were endorsing George Bush for president. Other conservatives might fall in line behind the candidacy of Bush, the incumbent president and Republican candidate for reelection, but not Ted. Under the rules adopted by the state Republican party, he had won election as a Buchanan delegate from the sixth congressional district in Massachusetts. This conservative young man complained that George Bush had betrayed the conservative cause. "It's time we had a leader who will do what the country needs," he said during an interview the next day at a downtown Houston hotel. He complained about Bush's ideology—the philosophical outlook that governed his actions: "I do not know where he stands."

Ted Maravelias stood out at the Republican National Convention because most of the conventioneers dutifully followed their leaders and endorsed Bush. But Maravelias' sentiments, similar to the beliefs and views that prompted Buchanan to challenge the incumbent president of his own party, were shared by many diehard conservatives. George Bush ended up losing control of the

National political conventions inspire the rank and file party faithful and deliver the party's first coherent message of the general election campaign. (Photo courtesy of the Bush Presidential Materials Project of the National Archives.)

Republican National Convention because of conservatives like Ted Maravelias. This loss of control would affect the outcome of the election.

PURPOSE OF CONVENTIONS

Control of the pictures and words emanating from a national convention is critically important because the conventions provide a unique opportunity to deliver a message to the American public. Party activists and political junkies dominate the primary and caucus season. It is not until convention time that many average people, who consider themselves too busy for politics earlier in the year, begin to tune in and pay attention to the presidential selection process. As recently as 32 years ago, the delegates to a national nominating convention actually picked the major party presidential and vice presidential nominees. In those times, a convention seethed with intrigue, back-stabbing, and double-dealing. In 1852, Franklin Pierce won the Democratic nomination in Baltimore after

49 roll calls. Franklin D. Roosevelt bested six other candidates to win the Democratic nomination after a 24-hour deadlock in 1932. He went on to win the presidency a record four times before the Constitution was changed to limit presidential terms to two.

Conventions have two official purposes: to nominate the presidential ticket and to adopt a party platform or statement of beliefs and principles. The 1960 conventions were the last ones in which there was any advance doubt about the identity of the party standard bearer. Since that time, the nominee has been known well in advance of the convention because the method for selecting delegates has shifted power to voters. Anyone can track the delegate count through the primary and caucus season and figure out who is ahead. As a result, some people have questioned the wisdom of conventions, costly four-day extravaganzas that seem to involve more party going than party building. They wonder why it is necessary for thousands of delegates to travel to a convention site, wear silly hats and goofy political buttons, and wave signs in front of television cameras just to ratify a foregone conclusion. In recent years, the national television networks even scaled back on their coverage of the national conventions because of the lack of news value.

Special Role of Conventions

Despite the lack of hard news value, national party conventions play a special role in the political process. They are a time to heal the wounds of the nominating season, to showcase the party nominee, to highlight the critical issues of the day in a way that favors the party, and to set the tone for the fall campaign. For the victors, they are great celebrations, a time to blow off steam and congratulate one another on a job well done before getting down to the gritty business of the general election campaign. For the losers, it is a time to forgive past slights, reconcile themselves to the loss, and get behind the winner. Conventions do not necessarily make or break a candidacy because months of campaigning remain before the November election, but they can create powerful impressions. The conventions may not hold much suspense about the nominee, but the potent mix of ingredients generates a political chemistry that produces unexpected developments.

Failed Conventions

Despite the best of intentions and planning, conventions can frequently deliver the wrong message. In 1964, the conservative forces then rising to power within the Republican party succeeded in nominating one of their own in San Francisco, Senator Barry Goldwater of Arizona. Goldwater's thundering acceptance speech sounded extremist to many voters, and Lyndon B. Johnson won the election in a huge landslide in November. The turmoil outside the Democrats' convention on the streets of Chicago in 1968 made the Democrats appear ineffective and weak at a time of great social turbulence and civil disobedience. The Democratic nominee, Hubert H. Humphrey who was Lyndon Johnson's vice president, never shook off the ill effects of the convention, and Republican Richard Nixon won in the fall. In 1972, the floor demonstrations at the Democratic Convention in Miami went on so long that George S. McGovern did not deliver his acceptance speech, his famous speech urging America to "Come home," until 2:48 a.m., long after the prime viewing time for the television audience. In 1980, the Democratic convention in New York only worsened the tension between the supporters of President Jimmy Carter and Senator Edward M. Kennedy who had unsuccessfully challenged Carter for the nomination. The party never truly solidified behind Carter, and this lack of support contributed to Carter's defeat in November.

EXPECTATIONS FOR THE CONVENTIONS IN 1992

In 1992, Bill Clinton and George Bush effectively won their respective party nominations months before the nominating conventions, but the conventions played a pivotal role in shaping the public perception of them and their political parties. The conventional wisdom would expect the Democrats to feature a wild and woolly convention because the greater diversity of its membership invites all sorts of unexpected consequences. Republicans, by contrast, are a smaller, more orderly, more homogeneous, and more disciplined party. The Democratic Convention in 1992 had 4,288 delegates, compared to 2,209 at the Republican Convention. Since 1968, the Republican National Conventions had been models of

Bill Clinton was the first candidate to make a brief appearance at the Democratic National Convention on the night of his nomination since John Kennedy in 1960. (Photo by Cable News Network, Inc., All Rights Reserved.)

clockwork efficiency while the Democratic Conventions often spun out of control.

The situation was just the opposite in 1992. Ronald H. Brown, the Democrats' party chairman, a cool and savvy politician whom Clinton later named commerce secretary, cracked his whip and pushed all of the ornery Democrats into line and ran what is regarded as the most successful Democratic Convention in modern times. His Republican counterpart, Richard Bond, a longtime Republican political operative who had worked on many of George Bush's political campaigns, lost control of his convention and the platform writing process to the most extremely conservative elements of the Republican party. The tone and rhetoric of the convention and the platform language alienated the so-called swing voters, the moderate suburbanites who swing one way or another depending upon the year and candidate. These voters had backed Bush in 1988 but switched to Clinton in 1992.

RULES FOR CAPTURING CONVENTION DELEGATES

The Democratic and Republican party rules for capturing convention delegates are different. The Republican rules favor incumbents like Bush and make it very difficult for an insurgent like Buchanan. For example, many states give the winner of a primary every single delegate vote from that state. This rule means that if a candidate won the primary by a single vote, the candidate received all of the state's delegates. This system is called "winner take all" and tends to make it easier for a front-runner to capture the nomination early in the primary process. Locking up the nomination early in the year is generally considered an advantage because it gives the Republican candidate more time to prepare his case against the Democrats for the general election. This system gave Bush a numerical advantage as early as Super Tuesday in mid-March that Pat Buchanan could not possibly overcome. Even though Buchanan stayed in the race for the entire nominating season and typically pulled a third of the vote in each contest, he wound up with only 78 delegates in the end.

The Democratic party rules call for distribution of delegates on the basis of the percentage of the vote won in the primary. This arrangement is called "proportional representation." If candidate X wins 30 percent of the vote, X gets approximately 30 percent of the delegates. This proportional distribution is why Jerry Brown went to the convention in New York with hundreds of delegates committed to his candidacy even though Clinton had effectively locked up the nomination after the New York primary election in early April. The modern Democratic party rules provide more opportunity for mischief because they allow room for more competing players. The Republican party is viewed by political professionals as almost royalist in nature, meaning that good Republicans are as likely to disagree in public with the party nominee as a loyal subject would challenge his king.

THE DEMOCRATIC NATIONAL CONVENTION

The Democratic National Convention, held for the third time since 1976 at Madison Square Garden in New York City, was an enormous political success for Bill Clinton and his party. While Ted Maravelias, the young Republican delegate mentioned at the beginning of this chapter, took pride in his unyielding conservatism ("I am," he said, "an unbending twig"), Democrats were in no mood to quibble about small differences after losing five of the last six presidential races. Years in the political wilderness wonderfully concentrated the collective party mind. Democratic activists were pleased by the choice of Gore and agog over the unusual energy generated by the two baby boomers on the same ticket. The Democratic Convention was designed to make the Democratic party look its best and to connect at an emotional level with average people.

In fact, average people participated in the convention proceedings via satellite. On Tuesday, the second day of the convention in New York, Holly Miller and Rico Bembry described the late night recreation center they opened in Seattle for young people to keep them away from drugs. Kyle Harrison and Louritha Green, two college students from Arkansas, talked about how financial aid was helping them stay in school. Ron and Rhonda Lee Machos of Manchester, New Hampshire, described how their health insurance was canceled after their baby son was born with a heart ailment.

Many politicians also shared personal stories. Governor Barbara Roberts of Oregon described how she got involved with politics in the 1960s. She was a divorced mom with two sons, one autistic. He was sent home from school because the public schools did not educate children with that disability then. "So I walked up the steps of the Oregon state Capitol, determined to change the law for kids like my son," she said. "I had absolutely no political experience, and I couldn't afford to buy even a cup of coffee for a member of the Oregon Legislature. But I knew that my cause was right and the rest I could learn, and I did. Five months later Oregon had a new law requiring education for disabled children, and I had a new direction." The convention cheered.

"I didn't start out to be a politician, but each of us is only one cause, one tragedy, one moral indignation away from political involvement," she said. "I found that one person could make a difference in politics, a positive difference for people, and I have never, never quit believing that . . . So I say to the men and women of America: Get involved."

Bill Clinton talked about the individuals who had influenced his life when he accepted his party's presidential nomination on the night of July 16, 1992 at Madison Square Garden. (Photo by Cable News Network, Inc., All Rights Reserved.)

Elizabeth Glaser, a young mother who had contracted the AIDS virus during a blood transfusion, spoke about how she unknowingly spread the infection to her two babies. Her little daughter had died already. She and her son were living under a death sentence. Delegates wept as they listened to her tragic story. "I am in a race with the clock," said this beautiful woman. "This is not about being a Republican or an Independent or a Democrat. It's about the future of each and every one of us."

Senator Barbara Mikulski of Maryland, the first Democratic woman ever elected to the U.S. Senate in her own right (she did not take the place of her husband), introduced six Democratic women who had won the U.S. Senate nominations in their states. Three of them would be elected in November. The diminutive senator with the big voice predicted that more women would join her in the U.S. Senate after the election.

"There will be a new vitality, a new heart and a new spirit, and a new way of doing business," she said. "Because we are women, we speak in a different voice and have a different perspective. A woman is not amazed to find out there are electronic scanners in the grocery store. A woman knows how to spell 'potato' because she buys them by the bag to stretch the family dollar. A woman knows that the country's problem is not a situation comedy created in Hollywood but an economic tragedy created in Washington."

Gore's Speech

The program was designed to show a contrast between the Republicans' and Democrats' policies and programs and exploit the problems of the nation in a way that benefited the Democratic ticket. Senator Al Gore, Clinton's vice presidential candidate, opened his acceptance speech by saying that he had dreamed since he was a boy growing up in Tennessee "that one day I'd have the chance to come here to Madison Square Garden and be the warm-up act for Elvis." (The traveling press corps had nicknamed Clinton "Elvis" after he serenaded them one night with some of his favorite rock star's hits.) Gore provided one of the convention's most emotional moments when he told how his six-year-old son Albert had almost died after being struck by a car after a Baltimore Orioles game just a few years earlier. He described how he ran to his son and lifted his limp body.

"His eyes were open, with the empty stare of death. And we prayed, the two of us there in the gutter, with only my voice," said the senator to a hushed crowd. "His injuries, inside and out, were massive. And for terrible days he lingered between life and death." His son recovered, but Gore added, "I came to tell you this straight from my heart. That experience changed me forever. When you have seen your six-year-old son fighting for his life, you realize that some things matter a lot more than winning." This touching story revealed another, more human side of Gore as a concerned father.

Introducing Clinton to Mainstream America

Beyond the emotional speeches, however the convention was supposed to be reintroducing Bill Clinton to the American public. The American public had heard George Bush speak many times on national television, but the Democratic National Convention would be the first time that most television viewers would hear Clinton speak at length despite his many appearances on talk shows. The convention is a time for symbolic acts, and Clinton had come to the convention hall the night before his acceptance speech to acknowledge the crowd right after the official roll call of the states gave him the nomination. He was the first candidate since John F. Kennedy to come to the convention before the final night, a similarity lost on no one. A film on Clinton produced by Hollywood producers Harry and Linda Bloodworth-Thomason, who were friends of the Clintons, told the story of his life in the most sympathetic light with Clinton on camera explaining his behavior and thinking.

Governor Ann Richards, the tart-tongued Texan who had delivered the convention keynote address four years earlier, introduced Clinton in a way that was intended to acknowledge that he had human failings. "Bill Clinton is not a creation of the media or of this party," she said. "He's not a cardboard-cutout candidate. He is a real human being."

When his turn came to address the convention, Clinton described the people who had taught him such as his grandfather and his mother and his wife.

"For too long those who play by the rules and keep the faith have gotten the shaft, and those who cut corners and cut deals have been rewarded," he said reprising the main theme of his middle-class-oriented campaign. "People are working harder than ever, spending less time with their children, working nights and weekends at their jobs instead of going to PTA and Little League or Scouts. And their incomes are still going down. Their taxes are still going up. And the costs of health care, housing, and education are going through the roof.

"Our people are pleading for change, but government is in the way. It has been hijacked by privileged private interests. It has forgotten who really pays the bills around here," he said. "We have got to go beyond the brain-dead politics in Washington and give our people the kind of government they deserve, a government that works for them."

He closed with a line that had been suggested by his wife. "My fellow Americans," he said, "I end tonight where it all began for me —I still believe in a place called Hope." Clinton was born in the tiny town of Hope, Arkansas.

Then the entire convention joined Jennifer Holliday, the Broadway soul singer; Reggie Jackson, a young black boy from

Florida with a clear beautiful voice; and Roger Clinton, Bill Clinton's younger half-brother, in singing "Circle of Friends." Thousands of Democrats who jammed every corner of the cavernous hall, swung together. When the convention adjourned at 11:44 p.m., the Fleetwood Mac song "Don't Stop Thinking about Tomorrow" showed more clearly than anything else that a new generation had taken charge.

Just six weeks earlier, Clinton had been in the political dumps running third behind Bush and Perot in the public opinion polls. But his concerted campaign to rebuild his public image through the so-called free media—free television appearances ranging from "Arsenio Hall" to "The Today Show" and "Larry King Live"—had worked well. He was on the way to political recovery in early July when he picked Senator Gore, of Tennessee, another young handsome baby boomer, to be his running mate. That choice injected the Democratic ticket with an extra jolt of energy. As a result, the Democrats gathered in New York in a celebratory mood. Although Jerry Brown still refused to endorse Clinton, the Democrats were amazingly unified. In a striking symbol of party unity, all but one of the Massachusetts convention delegates who were committed to the candidacy of their favorite son Paul Tsongas, switched and voted for Clinton during the roll call of the states. The lone holdout was a feisty former speaker of the Massachusetts House, an ex-Marine named Thomas McGee, who flat out refused to switch because Tsongas was his friend.

BUSH'S CAMPAIGN THROUGH THE REPUBLICAN NATIONAL CONVENTION

The Bush campaign also did Clinton a favor in June. While Clinton was crawling out of the basement of public opinion, the Bush forces concentrated their fire power on Perot and virtually ignored Clinton. At the same time, Bush still had problems with the most conservative members of his own party. Buchanan wanted a speaking role at the Republican National Convention, and Rich Bond said no way unless Buchanan withdrew as a candidate and endorsed Bush. Buchanan refused to accept these conditions so he remained in the race until the last bitter primary contest in June.

Two weeks before the final primary in California, Buchanan spoke one Saturday night to a meeting of California newspaper editors. His entourage had dwindled to two staff members, and after months of the road, he and his wife Shelley looked exhausted. The Secret Service protective detail seemed absurdly excessive given that he was attracting so little notice. He introduced his wife as the owner of "the most famous Mercedes Benz in America," the foreign car that had been the target of a Bush campaign ad during the Michigan primary campaign. During his speech, Buchanan described the high points of his campaign. His candidacy had put on the record an anti-Bush vote within the Republican party of about 30 percent. Whether Buchanan was on the ballot or not, whether he campaigned in a state or not, about one-third of the Republican primary voters pulled the lever for Buchanan in part to lodge a protest against Bush. This 30 percent represented the most conservative members of the Republican party. Buchanan took credit for forcing Bush to acknowledge that the nation was in an economic recession and that he had made a mistake when he raised taxes. He forced Bush to fire the head of the National Endowment of the Arts, a favorite target of the socially conservative Christian right wing. "There is alienation and anger out there in middle America," said Buchanan. "There is a sense of quiet desperation." He said that people who worked with their hands in manufacturing jobs were threatened by the North American Free Trade Agreement. Buchanan acknowledged that his relationship with Bush had deteriorated. And though he emerged from the process with fewer than 100 delegate votes out of more than 2,200 he said, "It was worth doing." He had no intention of withdrawing from the race he said. "One of the reasons I'm staying in this race is to try to influence this president, to bring attention to the issues," and then he added that he would speak at the convention, "If little Richard lets me in the building." He was referring to Rich Bond whom he had sarcastically once called a "coat holder," the demeaning term for a low-level political aide.

All this name calling and insulting only made relations worse between Buchanan and Bush, but a month before the convention, the political strategists in the Bush campaign began to worry about the conservatives who had voted for Buchanan. The Republican party needed to be completely unified after the convention in Houston because Clinton had left his convention in July far stronger than they had expected. Some quiet backdoor diplomacy began between Bay Buchanan, Pat's sister and campaign manager, and high-ranking representatives of the Bush campaign about a speaking role for her brother at the convention. He finally got his way, a prime time speaking slot just before former President Ronald Reagan on the opening night of the convention. Pat Robertson, the televangelist who had made an unsuccessful run for president in 1988, also got a prime time spot as did Marilyn Quayle, the wife of Vice President Dan Quayle. None of these speakers seemed out of the ordinary. What made this combination of speakers a huge problem for the Republicans was the tone and content of the speeches. By the end of the summer, the Bush campaign strategists realized that the Republican National Convention was the last and best opportunity to reverse the deterioration of the president's political standing. By August, Bush was in deep trouble. Clinton had made a dramatic recovery and moved ahead of him in the public opinion polls.

The Republican Reelection Theme and Preconvention Tone

The Bush team had a difficult time settling upon a theme for the reelection campaign. Vice President Dan Quayle tried to help out and in the spring introduced a theme of "family values" in a speech that criticized a character in a popular television situation comedy, "Murphy Brown." In this television show, the actress Candice Bergen played Murphy Brown, an unmarried network television journalist. During the 1992 television season, the character became pregnant and decided to have the baby on her own even though she was not married to the father. Quayle said that this choice demeaned the role of fathers and represented a selfish "lifestyle choice." Quayle's Murphy Brown speech opened Quayle to ridicule and brought criticism from single parents who accused the Republicans of being insensitive and intolerant of single parents who make up a large group in the United States. The theme of "family values" was a broad one, and, as defined by the most conservative Republicans, it celebrated a time when divorce was rare, when mothers stayed at home and cared for their children and did not work outside the home, and before minority groups demanded and received equal treatment and equal rights. Families were under severe stresses by 1992 because of changes in the economy and lifestyles and changes in the status of women. While some families were resilient and managed to thrive despite all these changes, others snapped and broke like brittle tree branches in an unforgiving wind. Broken marriages, alcoholism, drug abuse, and child abuse had become almost epidemic, and many Americans yearned for the good old days.

Days before the convention opened in Houston, Party Chairman Rich Bond charged that Hillary Clinton had compared marriage to slavery and wanted children to be able to sue their parents for higher allowances and more television time. This charge was a distortion of the truth. In scholarly legal articles she had written many years before, Hillary Rodham Clinton, a lawyer, had explained that women's legal standing in marriage before the laws were changed to guarantee women equal rights were that of a dependent, not an equal. In the law, this relationship was not unlike the one between a slave owner and a slave. She also had written that children who are beaten or sexually abused by their parents should have some legal way to get themselves out of the abusive situation so that they can be cared for by people who would not hurt them.

President George Bush and Vice President Dan Quayle and their wives accept the accolades of the convention delegates in Houston. (Photo courtesy of Cable News Network, Inc., All Rights Reserved.)

Bond's charges were part of a political strategy to exploit many people's anxieties about the changing roles of women in society. Hillary Clinton was a working mother and a partner in a major Little Rock law firm who was nationally known for her advocacy of children's rights. Because she believed firmly that women were equal to men and entitled to the same opportunities as men, she was targeted by conservatives who seemed to want to turn back the clock to 1950 before women entered the work force in large numbers as professionals. Earlier in the year during a debate before the Michigan and Illinois primary contests, Jerry Brown attacked Hillary Clinton because her law firm in Little Rock did some work for the state of Arkansas. Although Hillary Clinton had nothing to do with the state business, Brown said it was improper. In defending herself, Clinton said that she supposed she could have stayed home and baked cookies and held teas, but she had decided to fulfill her profession and practice law. This remark was widely viewed as a slap at the women who did choose to stay home and bake cookies. The changing roles of men and women in American society caused a lot of friction and anxiety, and her offhand remark drew a lot of criticism.

HOUSTON: THE REPUBLICAN CONVENTION

Rich Bond's criticism of Hillary Clinton set a negative tone for the Republican convention even before it officially opened. At the same time, representatives of the radical right wing of the Republican party were changing the party platform to be even more strongly opposed to legal abortion and affirmative action policies to benefit minorities and women. All of these developments were well publicized in the days leading up to what should have been a coronation of George Bush and a time to offer his view of where he wanted to lead the country during a second term. Instead, the convention got bogged down in criticism of Bill and Hillary Clinton. The problem for the Republicans is that millions of Americans interpreted this criticism as an attack on their own lifestyles and choices. Even some Republicans, particularly those who were homosexual or feminist or supporters of abortion rights, felt left out and unwanted.

Buchanan's Fire

Buchanan's speech on Monday night was vintage Buchanan. He beckoned fellow conservatives back into the Republican party family with a biting attack on Clinton and his wife. "The agenda Clinton & Clinton would impose on America, abortion on demand, a litmus test for the Supreme Court, homosexual rights, discrimination against religious schools, women in combat . . . is not the kind of change America needs," he said.

"There is a religious war going on in our country for the soul of America," he warned."It is a cultural war . . . and in that struggle for the soul of America Clinton and Clinton are on one side, and George Bush is on our side. And so, we have to come home and stand beside him." He described the Democratic National Convention as "a giant masquerade ball . . . where 20,000 radicals and liberals came dressed up as moderates and centrists in the greatest single exhibition of cross-dressing in American political history." He accused Clinton of being a draft dodger and said his foreign policy experience "is pretty much confined to having had breakfast once at the International House of Pancakes." He ridiculed Al Gore as "Prince Albert" and an environmental extremist. He accused Hillary Clinton of being a radical feminist. "Hillary believes that 12-year-olds should have a right to sue their parents, and she has compared marriage as an institution to slavery," he said repeating Rich Bond's attack. The harshness of this rhetoric shocked many television viewers.

The Quayles

While many viewers may not have agreed with all of Hillary Clinton's views, many women became angry because they felt that the Republicans were picking on her. In the 1960s, a majority of women stayed at home. In 1992, that number had reversed and a majority of women worked outside the home. Two nights later, Marilyn Quayle fueled the perception that the Republicans were intolerant of working women. The vice president's wife was a lawyer like Hillary Clinton, but she had stopped practicing law to stay home with her children and help her husband with his political career. In Washington, she was known as the vice president's most influential adviser, but in her speech she said that "most women do not want to be liberated from their essential natures as women." Mrs. Quayle and her husband were baby boomers like the Clintons, but she pointedly drew a contrast and said that not all baby boomers had joined the counterculture back in the 1960s. "Not everyone demonstrated, dropped out, took drugs, joined in the sexual revolution, or dodged the draft," she said in a way that criticized the millions who had. While Marilyn Quayle seemed more traditional than Hillary Clinton, in reality she was as influential and trusted an adviser to her husband as Clinton was to hers.

Vice President Quayle echoed much of his wife's sentiments when he, in his acceptance speech on Thursday night, said that the two political parties stood on different sides of a "cultural divide" and suggested that the Democrats were lacking in morals and patriotism. "All too often, parents struggle to instill character in their sons and daughters only to see their values belittled and their beliefs mocked by those who look down on America," he said. "Americans try to raise their children to understand right and wrong only to be told that every so-called lifestyle alternative is morally equivalent. That is wrong." These attacks were echoes of previous Republican charges that had hurt the Democrats in previous elections.

The world had changed since 1988, however, and the tactics that worked so well for the Republicans four years earlier when they demonized the Democratic opponent as a risky, unpatriotic liberal, no longer seemed to be effective. Voters were looking for some specific answers from the government and some economic relief, not more finger pointing. Working women who had a difficult time finding quality and affordable day care for their small children did not want politicians to make them feel more guilty about working outside the home; they wanted some help to make their lives easier and their children safer. The rhetoric of the Republican Convention not only insulted a lot of working women but failed to address their concerns.

Bush's Acceptance Speech

George Bush faced impossibly high expectations for his acceptance speech on the final night of the Republican Convention. All the pundits said he had to give the speech of his life. Most agreed that he rose to the occasion. Bush bashed Clinton for lacking character, and he trashed liberal Democrats for being wimpy on military and foreign policy. He blamed Democrats for the tax increase (the one he had signed as president). He offered an economic plan for his next term. He celebrated the astonishing fall of communism and changes taking place overseas, and took full credit for these foreign policy successes. "This convention is the first at which an American president can say the Cold War is over, and freedom finished first," Bush said. He mocked Clinton as "the leader of the Arkansas National Guard." He not so subtly noted that he had served in the military while Clinton had not. "While I bit the bullet, he bit his nails," said Bush.

He acknowledged that "this election is about change" but tried to turn the change theme to his advantage. "In this election, you'll hear two visions of how to do this," he said. "Theirs is to look inward, and protect what we already have. Ours is to look forward, to open new markets, prepare our people to compete, to restore our social fabric—to save and invest—so we can win. We believe that now that the world looks more like America, it is time for America to look more like herself. And so we offer a philosophy that puts

President Bush delivered a powerful speech, but it wasn't enough to win the election. (Photo by Cable News Network, Inc., All Rights Reserved.)

faith in the individual, not the bureaucracy," said Bush. "We start with a simple fact: Government is too big and spends too much."

Many observers commented that Bush's speech was like a Chinese menu: it offered something for everyone. But its political value may have lasted about as long as Chinese food. Within a remarkably short period of time, the public found itself ravenous for more policy meat than the skimpy outlines sketched out in Bush's speech.

The stakes for this Republican Convention had risen because of the success of the Democrats gathering in New York a month earlier. Ron Brown had hoped to make the Democratic convention a celebration of diversity, generational change, and the future. He succeeded. Just as the nomination of John F. Kennedy had symbolized a changing of the guard at the Los Angeles convention in 1960, so would the 1992 Democratic Convention seek to capitalize on the public's desire for change and the generational difference represented by the first baby boomer ticket in history. The Democrats also sought to make a virtue of their diversity. The official speakers included a gay man who had the virus that causes AIDS, six women who had just won U.S. Senate nominations, and an alphabet soup of politicians of different races and ethnic backgrounds.

When the hoopla in New York and Houston ended and the summer came to a close, the 1992 campaign was a two-man race between the incumbent president, George Bush, and the Democratic nominee, Bill Clinton. Ross Perot had withdrawn in July, and it would be another month before he would stun the political world with his surprise reentry. So the choice facing voters as the summer became fall was a stark one between the last president of the World War II generation who represented the status quo and a new candidate who represented the postwar baby boom generation and who was trying to convince voters that he represented the change they wanted.

Chapter 8

Perotmania: The Third Party Challenge

When Hollywood made a movie called *The Candidate,* the producers picked a young and handsome actor, Robert Redford, to play the title role of the ambitious but shallow politician who would do and say anything to be elected. In the movie Redford's character won the election and then, in the famous final scene, turned to his handlers and quizzically asked them, "What do I do now?" In 1992, the candidate who became the living symbol of voter discontent with the status quo was as different from that stereotypical blow-dried candidate as could be imagined. H. Ross Perot, the Texas businessman, seemed an unlikely person to run for president. He was a bantam-sized man with an old-fashioned crew cut and oversized ears that came to be carica-tured by hundreds of cartoonists. His Texas twang screeched like an out-of-tune guitar. Yet he drew more votes in the presidential election than any third party candidate in 80 years. Although he had never held public office, never so much as served on a local town board of selectmen, he received about one out of every five votes cast in the presidential election.

THIRD PARTY CHALLENGES TO THE TWO PARTY MONOPOLY

The Democratic and Republican parties have held a mo-nopoly on the American presidency since 1860. But third parties, driven by racial discord, economic distress, and ideology, have played a lively supporting role and frequently been the grassroots pressure that forced the major parties to deal with touchy issues including slavery and extending the vote to women. The issue in 1992 was the economy.

As a self-made billionaire businessman, Perot had credibility when he chided both the Democrats and Republicans for their unwillingness to confront the dangers of a staggeringly huge budget deficit, national debt, and trade imbalance. Perot initially did not think of himself as the candidate type, but he was the prototype of the American folk hero. The firestorm he unleashed on Larry King's call-in show on Cable News Network in late February (when he said he might run if his name got on every state ballot) swept him and his followers along in a historic gush of democratic action.

From the start, Perot faced long odds because American politics has tended to break into two warring camps since the earliest days of the republic when the Federalists and the Jeffersonian Republicans fought over how power should be divided between the national government and individuals. The Federalists became the Whigs who became the Republican party by the time of the 1860

Ross Perot's appearance on "Larry King Live" on Cable News Network in late February sparked a grassroots effort to persuade the Texas billionaire to run for president. (Photo by Cable News Network, Inc. All Rights Reserved.)

presidential election with Abraham Lincoln as the presidential candidate. The Jeffersonian Republicans became the Jacksonian Democrats and then just plain old Democrats. Today the Republicans tend to be more conservative and the Democrats more liberal, but both parties include both conservative and liberal members.

The major political parties are most successful when they offer a mainstream platform that appeals to a broad cross section of Americans. If a party moves too far to the right as the Republican party did in 1964 with the nomination of Barry Goldwater or too far to the left as the Democratic Party did in 1972 with the nomination of George McGovern, then they lose the people in the middle who actually decide presidential elections—the so-called swing voters. Throughout American history, third political parties have either been driven by economic conditions or a specific ideological agenda. As a result, these parties tend to fall at one extreme or the other. The Liberty party, established in the 1840s, was the first antislavery party in the United States. It eventually was displaced by the Free Soil party, which was absorbed by the Republican party by 1860. The Greenbacks, an uprising of disgruntled farmers, became the People's party or Populists who ended up getting submerged by the Democrats when the Democrats chose William Jennings Bryan, a candidate who championed the Populists' agenda, to be their presidential nominee in 1896. This tendency to co-opt the opposition by adopting its positions when those positions became popular is one of the reasons the two major political parties have been so enduring.

Previous Third Party Challenges

Unsuccessful presidential candidates have spun off their own political parties to mount third party candidacies in November after losing their party nominations. Theodore Roosevelt lost the Republican nomination in 1912 and promptly established the Bull Moose party. His presence on the ballot split the vote and led to a Democratic victory that year, Woodrow Wilson winning the election. A group of Southern Democrats spun off into the State's Rights Democratic party in 1948 in protest over President Harry Truman's civil rights proposals. The Dixiecrats, as they called themselves, nominated Strom Thurmond, the Democratic governor of South Carolina, to be their presidential nominee. Thurmond eventually switched parties and became a Republican U.S. senator. The same racial tensions led to a third party candidacy 20 years later of George Wallace, the Democratic governor of Alabama. Wallace made little headway in the 1968 Democratic primaries campaigning against civil rights laws and the impasse in Vietnam, and so he ran as an American party candidate in November. He won 14 percent of the vote, helping Richard Nixon secure the victory.

THE 1992 CAMPAIGN: FERTILE GROUND FOR A THIRD PARTY CHALLENGE

Third parties tend to do best at times of discontent with the major political parties and when headed by a well-known figure, and so the seeds of Perot's candidacy fell upon fertile territory in 1992. Millions of voters were disgusted with the gridlock between the Democrats and Republicans in Washington and blamed both parties equally. Although Perot was not a household name at the beginning of the year, he was better known than many businessmen; he had almost unlimited money so he could make himself as well known as the major party candidates through paid television advertising and use of the free media in a year when the talk shows became a major way to communicate directly with the people. Television proved to be an especially effective medium for a man like Perot who literally talked in sound bites. Perot was blunt, funny, and folksy and made complicated issues seem simple, even issues like the national debt. "The debt," he said, "is like a crazy aunt we keep down in the basement. All the neighbors know she's there, but nobody wants to talk about her."

Perot's Entry, Withdrawal, and Reentry into the Race

Perot had appeared to be moving inexorably towards a presidential run throughout the spring of 1992 as his grassroots supporters gathered signatures on petitions to get his name on state ballots. His abrupt decision not to run in July, announced on the day that Bill Clinton accepted the Democratic Party's presidential nomination, threw his supporters into turmoil. Many felt betrayed by their

Ross Perot howled with laughter when a volunteer in Massachusetts presented him with these rubber waders to protect him from the Washington "doo doo" at a rally on the historic Boston Common in June. (Photo by Barry Chinn, *Boston Globe.*)

champion, but a surprising number of the Perot followers stayed together and continued to work to get him on the ballot and to support candidates who supported the issues that he highlighted.

Perot had been embarrassed in the spring because he could identify the nation's problems easy enough, but he did not have any real answers. In response, he hired a high-powered staff headed by

John White, an executive with Eastman Kodak Co., to develop some answers for him. The economic program was turned into a paperback book called *United We Stand, America: How We Can Take Back Our Country*. The book contained a lot of unpopular proposals including higher taxes on gasoline, but it hit the best-seller list because Americans were hungry for straight talk and real answers.

By September, it had become clear that Perot was inching towards an "October surprise" and a reentry into the race. In July he said he absolutely would not run for president, but by early September he had changed his rhetoric. He went on "CBS This Morning" and said that quitting the race had been a mistake. He placed his fate into the hands of his volunteer supporters. "We felt very strongly that we should give both parties a chance to face the issues," he said on the morning news show. "In retrospect, I think I made a mistake because they really didn't face the issues. But it's all in the hands of volunteers, they're evaluating it now." Representatives of Clinton and Bush traveled to Dallas to make presentations to Perot's volunteers and woo their support. Each side claimed to be closer to Perot's views than the other. Both sides were criticized for pandering to Perot. Not surprisingly, Perot's loyalists stuck with him. He had been supporting the grassroots organizations and spent $16 million during the summer and early fall when he was allegedly not running for president. He also conducted a telephone poll with a toll-free 800 number to assess the opinion of his supporters on whether or not he should run. The outcome, however, was never in doubt. The "poll" automatically counted every single one of the 1.5 million calls as a "yes" vote for Perot to run.

Perot II

Perot II was launched on October 1 for a 33-day campaign that brought Perot unprecedented public attention for a third party candidate. He was included in the three nationally televised presidential debates, and he dipped into his fortune to make unprecedented expenditures on television time by an independent presidential candidate. From the start, Perot was determined to run for president his way or no way. This "campaign" was largely run from a television studio where his message could be carefully packaged and controlled without any interference from either voters or the press. Perot was such a novelty that he attracted heavy news coverage from the television networks and major newspapers that immediately posted correspondents to Dallas to cover the action. The talk shows were delighted to have him as a guest. He, like all the candidates who made such appearances in 1992, was good for ratings.

During an appearance on the "Today Show" on NBC, he did his own marketing and plugged his upcoming 30-minute infomercial on jobs and the economy. Perot bragged that he wrote the show himself. He said that voters were sick and tired of superficial negative TV commercials. He vowed to run an issue-oriented campaign. "I can't be a spoiler," he told Bryant Gumbel, the "Today Show" co-host. "There is no way I can be a spoiler. It was already spoiled when I started. I'm just a clean-up man."

Perot had had a falling out with the professional political operatives whom he had hired to run his campaign back in the spring. He did not like being told what to do. Orson Swindle, the former military man who was head of the volunteer organization United We Stand, and Sharon Holman, Perot's longtime publicist and aide, were acting as the representatives for the campaign in the absence of anyone else, although they were often unaware of what Perot was doing or thinking. Perot was truly a one-man band.

Swindle did the best he could to explain why so many Americans were drawn to Perot's quirky candidacy. "We are approaching this thing as forthrightly as we know how to do it," he explained one morning at the daily briefing for the national press. "We are gravely concerned about the future of this country and the problems we have before us which no one seems to want to tackle or even address.

"The American people are disgusted," said Swindle. "I think we have just about had enough. The more enlightened we become, the more empowered we want to be. The more empowered we are, the better we can carry out steps to correct the frustrations that are within us. We are a frustrated nation. We have got $4 trillion worth of debt and basically not a damn thing to show for it."

Infomercials

The first Perot infomercial aired on October 6 on network television. Perot called it "Jobs, Debt and the Washington Mess." The broadcast and its success flipped the conventional wisdom on its head. Media consultants thought that most voters had the attention span of a toddler and recommended that politicians deliver their messages in small-sized sound bites. But Perot's show ran for a full 30 minutes. Instead of pretty pictures, emotional music, and safe cliches, the broadcast featured Perot sitting at a desk, armed with a silver pointer and dozens of pie charts, as he explained the nation's economic difficulties.

"We used to have the world's greatest economic engine, we let it slip away and with it went millions of jobs and taxpayers," he explained. "Let's take a little time and figure out what happened to the engine. Let's raise the hood and go to work. Let's diagnose the problem. I can tell you before we look at the engine, an engine tune-up won't fix it. We're gonna have to do a major overhaul."

Perot pulled out a chart to show the growth of the national debt to more than $4 trillion. "It's like the guy who went into the hospital—thought he had a sore arm—found out he had gangrene," he said in his folksy way. "Everybody west of the Mississippi that sends income taxes into the Internal Revenue Service—their taxes are used just to pay interest on the federal debt. They don't buy anything for you; they don't buy anything for your children. . . . We've got to cut it out."

He pulled out another chart to show the growth of federal spending. He said that the politicians in Washington had lost touch with the people because of the perquisites that accompany power such as free parking at National Airport and a subsidized barber at the Capitol.

Then Perot showed more charts that demonstrated the link between consumer spending, industrial production, and payroll employment. "We got into trickle-down economics and it didn't trickle," he said indicting the philosophical underpinning of the Reagan and Bush years.

"Most of the jobs we created in the last 12 years are minimum wage jobs," he said. "They just don't support a family. They just don't support our country. We've got to go back to building and making things."

"This has not been pleasant for you I know," he said at the end. "This possibly comes as a shock to you. But, please, step one—we decided we'd look under the hood and decide what we had to do. We've looked under the hood. We now know what we have to do. The next step is let's just do it."

The show could have been called Economics 101. It was serious and substantive as Perot carefully walked viewers through the economic trends of the past 12 years. Yet it turned out to be a political smash hit. More than 16 million viewers tuned in to watch Professor Perot. He attracted more viewers than the National League baseball playoffs that followed him on the air. From a political standpoint, the show helped Perot improve his own standing with voters who had lost faith with him when he quit the race in July.

There was another political dimension to this broadcast, however. Perot was doing just what Pat Buchanan did earlier in the year. He was helping the Democratic ticket by acting as a third party critic of the incumbent Bush administration and a credible one at that. While many Americans might not view Perot as a president, just as many Republican voters did not see Buchanan as a president, he was considered a serious and knowledgeable person whose critique of the Bush administration had real bite. Everyone watching knew that Perot was a billionaire and could have anything money could buy. When he denounced trickle-down economics for being unfair, it meant more than if the same words came from a liberal Democratic politician who had never had a job in the private sector. Perot was seen as a reliable source of information.

Perot as Truth Teller

Perot, like Buchanan, Tsongas, and Brown, emerged as one of the most potent truth tellers of the 1992 campaign. His candidacy showed very clearly that a candidate for the presidency need not win the election to have an impact on the nation. Months later when President Clinton was selling his economic plan to the nation, a plan that called for sacrifice from many Americans, he was building upon a foundation built in part by Perot in his famous infomercials. Thanks to the truth tellers who taught the public about the dangers of a huge national debt and the risks of endless deficit spending, citizens better understood the issues that Clinton faced as president. Perot had none of the conventional advisers of a candidate. "He is not being prepped, poised, perfumed, or coifed," said Sharon Holman of her boss when reporters wanted to know how he was preparing for the debates. "That is what the American people want," said Swindle. "They are tired of the tinsel and paste."

Perot at the Debates

The Bush campaign had insisted that Perot be included in the three presidential debates. Office holders rarely want to debate their opponents because it not only gives the opposition public exposure and an opportunity to lay a good punch on them in public, but it also elevates the status of the challenger to that of an equal. Frontrunners never want to debate for the same reason. Bush, however, was trailing in the polls, and in September his campaign strategists realized that they needed to do something dramatic to change the dynamic of race. So after months of refusing to set a date for a debate, the Bush team abruptly challenged Clinton to four debates. During negotiations they insisted that Perot be included, apparently reasoning that a one-on-one confrontation between Bush and Clinton was not to Bush's advantage.

But at the first debate on a Sunday night in St. Louis, the decision to include Perot began to look like a big mistake. Perot wasted no time in brandishing his unconventional qualifications for the presidency. "I don't have any experience in running up a $4 trillion debt. I have no experience in gridlock government. I do have a lot of experience in getting things done," he said showing that he was a can-do businessman, not a conventional politician. Just as his first infomercial had indirectly helped Clinton by criticizing the policies of the Reagan and Bush years, Perot made statements that undermined the Bush attacks on Clinton's character. Asked about character, Perot thoughtfully said that he believed there was a big difference between what one did as a young man and what one did as a senior government official. It was worse to him that a senior government official would refuse to take responsibility for the consequences of his policies than the indiscretions of youth. He was drawing a clear cut moral difference between Clinton's youthful attempts to evade the draft and Bush's present behavior as president.

Perot said, "We've created a mess and don't have much to show for it." Off-camera in the makeshift television studio at Washington University in St. Louis, Clinton nodded energetically in agreement.

"I'm not playing Lawrence Welk music here tonight," said Perot after explaining why it was necessary to increase the taxes on gasoline. "It's now time to pay the fiddler. We've got to clean this mess up." Again Clinton was nodding vigorously in agreement.

"We practice nineteenth-century capitalism," said Perot whose credentials as a capitalist were impeccable. "The rest of the world practices twenty-first-century capitalism."

He said that he had no patience with plans and commissions and studies. "My orientation is let's go do it," he said.

Instant polls conducted for all three networks after the broadcast showed Perot was seen as the winner of the debate and more voters were likely to vote for him before than after. But at this juncture, Perot's words and actions suggested strongly that the true purpose of this effort was not so much to win but to influence the political debate and force Clinton and Bush to confront the difficult economic issues. Perot held a press conference after the first debate in St. Louis, his first since reentering the race almost two weeks earlier. He seemed amazed that he had been allowed to participate in the debate at all. "I'm surprised they let me show up," he said. Winning was not what this was all about he said. "This is not my life's mission. My life will not come to a screeching halt if they do not vote for me. The main thing I want to try to do is make sure we face the issues. By election day, there may not be a dime's worth of difference in the three platforms. The real issue is, are we going to do something about it or just talk about it?"

Perot had taped a second 30 minute infomercial laying out his plan for solving the nation's economic difficulties. Some commentators predicted that his popularity would wane when voters understood that his solutions called for sacrifice. He held back on airing the solutions show until after the first debate. The solutions show followed the same format as the first. This time Perot replaced his silver pointer with a voodoo stick that had been sent to him by a supporter. "It is voodoo economics and maybe now is the time for me to wave the voodoo stick and get rid of the hex," he said. This lecture was no feel-good political commercial. He described the United States as a failing economic power and warned that only drastic action would curb the decline and put the United States on the road to economic recovery. "We better get busy and start rebuilding our great country and not just wandering around and saying 'Well, everything will work out if we don't do anything,'" he said. He called for long-term thinking and an investment strategy that would pay off in the future not just in time for a quarterly dividend payment for stockholders.

His solutions included a 50 cent increase per gallon in the federal gas tax over the next five years, higher business taxes, higher tobacco taxes, higher income taxes for the wealthiest four percent, a limit on home mortgage deductions to one $250,000 home, cuts in government programs, higher Medicare premiums, and higher taxes on the wealthiest Social Security recipients. "We have got to collect more taxes in this country," Perot said, "And this is one fair place to get it if we spend all of that money on building for the future and don't squander it on some new pork barrel program in Congress."

Perot stressed that action was needed. "The thing we can't do is just sit here playing Lawrence Welk music, 'Wonderful, Wonderful, Wonderful,' and doing nothing. We've got to start moving," he said. (Lawrence Welk was a band leader from Perot's generation who hosted a television entertainment show.) "We can be a country leading the way instead of a country falling behind," he said. ". . . if we will make the tough choices today."

Biographical Infomercials

While the Perot effort in October had begun as an attempt to focus the two major party candidates on the economic issues, it started to veer off track by the third week. The scholarly content of the infomercials suddenly switched from promoting serious issues to promoting Perot and his sanitized and idealized version of his humble background. A longtime associate who was on his payroll,

Murphy Martin, "interviewed" Perot as he gave these valentines to himself. For the first 30-minute biographical broadcast, a folksy Perot rambled about his boyhood in Texarkana. He said he learned his business training at the knee of his father, a cotton broker. "He was my best friend," said Perot. He described his mother as "a saint. Nobody could have had a better mother." He explained how his father sold his horse one day during the Depression in order to buy Christmas gifts for Perot and his sister. Perot described himself as a Horatio Alger type of youngster who made money by breaking horses, selling magazines and cards, and delivering newspapers even to the poor section of town. He talked about how he had stood up for principle as the president of the student council at Texarkana Junior College, his experiences in the Naval Academy and as a young Navy officer, his first blind date with the girl who became his wife, and his first big job at IBM.

The danger of selling himself instead of selling his economic message is that Perot, his character and his temperament became the issue. Though it is important to note that the voters elect a

Volunteer in Massachusetts worked the phones to recruit more supporters for their favored candidate in late June just after Perot appeared in the state. (Photo by Tom Herde, *Boston Globe*.)

person to be president, not just a set of ideas or a platform, Perot's selling of himself left him open to criticism. He had displayed a pattern throughout his life of seeing anyone who crossed him as an enemy. He brought lawsuits against business competitors when he lost a contract because he was convinced that he could not ever lose on the merits. He was suspicious of his associates and had hired private investigators to investigate his employees and even a boyfriend of one of his daughters. During the third presidential debate, Perot startled the audience by claiming that his life had been threatened by North Vietnamese Communists and drug dealers because of his work on behalf of American prisoners of war and his role in an anti-drug campaign in his native Dallas.

Perot and the Media

As Perot began to break out of the protective cocoon he had built around his candidacy and move into more conventional type of campaign activities such as television interviews, he began to self-destruct. For the first few weeks of this campaign, he remained in seclusion in Dallas surrounded only by people on his payroll as he taped his television commercials. He made no public appearances outside of a TV studio. He flew in a private jet from Dallas to each of the debate sites in St. Louis, Richmond, and East Lansing, and flew back the very same night not even staying overnight in another city. But as he ventured outside of the carefully controlled atmosphere of the television studio, Perot began to behave in a way that raised questions about his temperament, stability, and ability to hold the office of president. After the final debate in East Lansing, he opened a press conference in nearby Lansing by attacking the reporters without any provocation. He called them "jerks," effectively told respected *New York Times* reporter Steven Holmes that he was stupid, and told the *Time Magazine* correspondent that his magazine was "a joke."

"You boys have less respect in this country than Congress," he sneered to the stunned reporters who had not yet had a chance to ask him any questions. "I think you would do anything to get a gotcha story, anything to get a headline, get you a story, get a bonus, get among your peers and do a high five and get on the front page and be a big man. I think you have enormous responsibilities under the

First Amendment that you do not discharge. You guys just hate the fact that I am in this race. You hate the fact that the American people put me on the ballot."

Perot's Charges of Republican "Dirty Tricks"

The situation worsened when Perot made unsubstantiated charges against the Republican party. During an interview on the CBS news show "60 Minutes" on Sunday, October 25, just ten days before the election, he claimed that Republican dirty tricks had forced him out of the presidential race in July. To an incredulous interviewer, Leslie Stahl, Perot said that Republicans intended to embarrass his youngest daughter with a computer-modified photograph that showed her in a compromising position and by disrupting her August wedding. He also claimed that he understood that a CIA contract employee met with high-ranking Republican officials to wiretap code numbers used by his corporation when it dealt with international financial markets to ruin him financially. Republicans immediately dismissed the charges as "preposterous." Reporters scrambled to find out if the charges were true. Perot openly acknowledged that he did not have a single shred of evidence to back up his allegations just as he had no evidence to support his claims that he had been the target of North Vietnamese Communists and drug dealers.

The allegations raised more questions about Perot's behavior and temperament than they did about any Republican predilection to pull dirty tricks. There was some irony in that the characteristics that made him a successful businessman, the single-minded ruthlessness, the suspicion of competitors, and the other characteristics that made him a compelling individual also gave him an unusually high self-destruct quotient for a political candidate. Daily tracking polls showed that Perot picked up support between the first debate on Sunday, October 11, and the third debate on Monday, October 19. Because he had nothing to lose, he could say just what he pleased, a luxury that neither Bush nor Clinton had. But the debit column was mounting at the same time. The befuddled debate performance of Perot's vice-presidential candidate James Bond Stockdale had troubled many voters. (See Chapter 9 for a more detailed description.) Now Perot himself was ringing alarm bells among citizens who may have liked what he said but wanted to be sure that the next president would be able to govern effectively. Perot's lone ranger style raised questions about whether he could engage in the give-and-take that is a crucial part of governing.

On the previous Friday, the day he taped the "60 Minutes" interview, Perot had made the same allegations of dirty tricks to the startled editorial board of the *Boston Herald*. The *Herald* editorial board had flown to Dallas to interview Perot because the newspaper was considering endorsing his candidacy. The newspaper ran a story about his remarks on Sunday morning, the same day as the "60 Minutes" broadcast. When a copy of the front page article was relayed to the Clinton campaign headquarters in Little Rock by facsimile that day, George Stephanopoulos, the communications director for Clinton, pushed it across his desk to a reporter. His fatigue from a long campaign and the tension of the final 10 days showed in the lines that crossed his young face on this Sunday afternoon, but his face broke into a broad smile as he handed over the facsimile copy. The Clinton campaign strategists believed that the lone ranger from Texas had finally shot himself in the foot.

Chapter 9

The Second Banana: Vice President

The vice presidency of the United States, the second highest job in the U.S. government, has often been denigrated, its occupant mocked or ignored. John Adams, the first vice president, described the position as "the most insignificant office that ever the invention of man contrived or his imagination conceived." John Nance Garner, the vice president between 1933 and 1941, likened the job to a "warm bucket of spit." But five of last ten presidents of the United States once served as vice president. The vice presidency is the single most important stepping stone to the presidency. In the event of the death, disability, or resignation of the president, the second banana automatically becomes the president.

In the last 50 years, three vice presidents were elevated to the presidency without warning. Vice President Harry S. Truman became president when Franklin D. Roosevelt died in 1945. Vice President Lyndon B. Johnson took the oath of office on an Air Force jet in Dallas, Texas, just hours after the assassination of John F. Kennedy in 1963. And Vice President Gerald R. Ford became president when the Watergate scandal forced Richard M. Nixon to resign on a hot summer day in 1974. Ford, the former Republican leader in the House, was a fill-in vice president, selected by Nixon after the elected vice president, Spiro T. Agnew, was forced to resign.

ROLE OF THE VICE PRESIDENT

Although the position has frequently been demeaned, the vice presidency has given its occupants public exposure and experience that translates into an advantage in running for the presidency. Seven of the last ten vice presidents sought and won their party's presidential nominations. The founding fathers created the position of vice president almost as an afterthought to deal with the problem of succession in the event of the sickness, death, or impeachment of the president.

The impeachment process is the only way a president can be removed from office during his term. If the president breaks the law, betrays his country, or commits some other serious offense that would make him unfit to serve as president, the Congress brings charges and conducts a trial. If the Senate finds him guilty, he is removed from office. Presidents have been impeached, but no president has ever been convicted by the Senate. After the House voted to impeach Nixon, he resigned on August 9, 1974, to avoid a trial by the Senate. In 1868 the house impeached President Andrew Johnson after he tried to fire the secretary of war, but he was acquitted or found not guilty by the Senate.

From the start, the vice president had two jobs—to preside over the U.S. Senate and vote in the event of a tie and to take over the presidency in the event the president was no longer able to perform his duties. The responsibilities of the office remain the same today more than 200 years later, but over the years the method for selecting vice presidents has changed along with the prestige of the position. At first, the presidential candidate who ran second to the winner in the electoral college balloting (the primary method for presidential selection before the popular vote) would be the vice president. This rule assured that the vice president would be of the same quality, stature, and experience as the president.

But over time, the method of selection changed as did the quality of the vice presidents. The original method for selecting vice presidents soon proved problematic because competitors for the presidency would end up serving together in a kind of shotgun marriage. The growth of political parties that held different points of view made this particularly awkward. A president and a vice president from different political parties often found themselves working at cross purposes. Eventually through constitutional amendments the process was changed so that the president and vice president run together as a team on the same ticket. The presumption was that two members of the same political party would share the same views and be able to work together. This change was also an attempt to guarantee that the public will would not be frustrated in the event of an emergency. A vice president elected on the same ticket as the president and picked by him would presumably continue the policies which that president was elected to implement. The 25th Amendment to the U.S. Constitution, ratified by the states in 1967, governs presidential succession. The amendment says that whenever the presidency becomes vacant, the vice president automatically becomes president. If the president becomes temporarily disabled because he undergoes surgery or is in an accident, the 25th Amendment allows the vice president to become "acting president" until the president can resume his duties. That amendment also allows the president to appoint a new vice president with the approval of Congress.

Balancing the Ticket

But these changes also tended to reduce the importance of the vice president. At national nominating conventions, presidential candidates and their advisers became more concerned with picking a vice presidential candidate who could improve the ticket's chances of winning the election than in picking a candidate who would make a good president. More often than not, political expediency dictated the choice of vice president. John N. Garner, the Speaker of the U.S. House and a savvy Texas politician, had no desire to be vice president at all. But after he threw the support of the Texas delegation behind Franklin D. Roosevelt at the Democratic convention in 1932, support that gave Roosevelt the presidential nomination, he was persuaded to take the second spot to help the ticket in the South. In 1960, John F. Kennedy, a Massachusetts senator, picked his rival for the presidency, Senator Lyndon B. Johnson of Texas, to be his running mate even though many of the

Kennedy staffers hated Johnson. Johnson helped Kennedy to win votes in the South just as Garner had helped Roosevelt who was the governor of New York when he ran for the presidency. In 1980, Ronald Reagan picked his principal competitor for the presidency, George Bush, even though many of his top advisers, particularly the strong conservatives, were horrified because Bush had dismissed Reagan's central political pitch as "voodoo economics." Reagan reasoned that picking Bush would make it easier for him to unite the Republican party after a divisive primary campaign.

Ticket balancing became a political art. Presidential candidates often picked vice presidents with characteristics they lacked. Geography, gender, experience, and political considerations came into play. A westerner, like Reagan, might pick an easterner, like Bush. A Washington outsider like Jimmy Carter who had been the governor of Georgia picked a U.S. senator with extensive Washington experience, Walter F. Mondale from Minnesota. Mondale, the 1984 Democratic presidential nominee, picked the first woman in history to run on a major party ticket, Congresswoman Geraldine Ferraro from New York City. A vice president candidate coming from a big populous state became a more important factor than the vice president's ability to perform the duties of the presidency. When political columnist Jules Witcover wrote a book on the haphazard vice presidential selection process, he called it: "Crapshoot: Rolling the Dice on the Vice Presidency."

The vice president has frequently been unprepared to assume the presidency, in large part because most presidents had little inclination to share power with another person, particularly someone who might surface someday as a potential political rival. Harry Truman, a onetime haberdasher who had served in the U.S. Senate, had been vice president only 82 days when Franklin D. Roosevelt died, and he was thrust into the office. During his time as vice president, Truman had barely seen President Roosevelt who was out of the country for much of that time. Truman had never even met the secretary of state, the cabinet secretary in charge of dealing with foreign nations. This was at a time when World War II was still underway. Truman was open about how overwhelmed he felt. After leaving a lunch with friends in Congress, he told a group of reporters: "Boys, if you ever pray, pray for me now. I don't know whether you fellows ever had a load of hay fall on you, but when they told me yesterday what had happened, I felt like the moon, the stars, and all the planets had fallen on me."

Political Significance of the Vice President

The political significance of the vice president is a matter of considerable debate within the political community. Public opinion polls conducted during recent presidential campaigns seem to show that voters are far more concerned about the presidential candidate than the vice presidential candidate. The conventional wisdom is that vice presidents do not help much but can hurt a lot. As a result, candidates usually try to pick someone who is not controversial. In 1988, Governor Michael S. Dukakis picked Senator Lloyd M. Bentsen of Texas to be his running mate, a replica of the Boston-Austin axis that worked for Kennedy and Johnson 28 years earlier. Bentsen, a highly regarded and senior senator, was regarded as a solid choice. In fact, by the end of the campaign some Democrats were privately saying that Democratic chances of winning the election would improve if Dukakis and Bentsen switched places. From a political standpoint, however, while Bentsen did not hurt Dukakis, he did not seem to help him much either. Bentsen was running simultaneously for reelection to the U.S. Senate and for vice president in 1988. He easily won reelection to the Senate in Texas, but his presence on the Democratic presidential ticket was not enough to convince a majority of Texans to vote for Dukakis for president. Bush carried the state.

DAN QUAYLE

The Dukakis campaign tried to make an issue of the thin qualifications of Bush's vice president, James Danforth Quayle III, a youthful and junior senator from Indiana, with negative television commercials. One ad ominously featured the beating of a heart to symbolize that Quayle would be a heartbeat away from the presidency, but the polling conducted for Dukakis' own campaign showed that only the most partisan Democrats were upset over the selection of Quayle. These Democrats intended to vote for

Dukakis regardless of Quayle so Quayle was not the drag on the Republican ticket that the Democrats had hoped he would be.

Bush, vice president to Ronald Reagan for eight years, shocked even his close friends when he picked Dan Quayle to be his running mate in 1988 at the Republican National Convention in New Orleans. Bush picked Quayle because he and some of his advisers thought that Quayle would appeal to conservatives because he had compiled a very conservative record in the Senate and would appeal to women because he was young and good-looking. The nation's first look at the candidate came when the 41-year-old Quayle, giddy with joy, bounded up to Bush like a puppy dog, and grabbed the very surprised Bush in an awkward bear hug on a riverboat in New Orleans. First impressions in politics can be lasting, and Quayle's first impression did not inspire confidence.

As the national press corps scrambled for background information on the man whom Bush proposed to be the second in command,

Charles Gibson of ABC's "Good Morning America" interviews Vice President Dan Quayle. The vice president's tendency to make mistakes made the Bush campaign strategists nervous about his network television appearances. (Photo by Capital Cities/ABC Inc.)

a succession of damaging disclosures came out. Quayle, a member of a wealthy publishing family in Indiana, had not done well in college but was accepted into law school because of an affirmative action program intended to help poor minority group members. The most damaging story alleged that he pulled strings and used his family's influence to avoid service in Vietnam by getting a spot in the Indiana National Guard. Very few national guard units were ever called up for combat service in Vietnam. The guard was widely used as a way for draft eligible men to meet their national service requirements but avoid the risks of combat. As these stories came out, it became hard for people to take Quayle seriously, especially in light of the first impression he gave voters on the riverboat. Soon even the mention of his name was enough to draw hilarious laughter from audiences. He became the favorite target of late night television comics.

Quayle did not make things any easier on himself. One day in Chicago, resentful of the professional political consultants who were trying to improve his public image, he discarded the speech on foreign policy they had prepared for him and spoke off the cuff. His rambling, at times incomprehensible, remarks relied upon the philosophy of a university basketball coach and a fictitious scenario from a best-selling thriller to back up his views. He often mangled his words. He once boosted Bush's proposal for helping parents obtain child care through a system of tax credits by saying, "We understand the importance of the bondage between parent and child." He meant to say bonding. Sometimes he made no sense at all. One day Quayle described the Holocaust, the horrible period when Nazi Germany systematically attempted to eradicate Jews and others who did not conform to the Aryan ideal as "an obscene period in our nation's history." When he was corrected, he became even more confused and said, "Our nation was on the side of justice . . . I mean, we, we all lived in this century. I didn't live in this century, but in this century's history."

The most devastating blow came during the vice presidential debate with Senator Bentsen, a courtly and distinguished older man whom Clinton later chose to be his treasury secretary. Quayle often compared himself to John F. Kennedy, a Democrat, even though he was a Republican. During the debate he asserted that he had as much experience as John Kennedy did when he sought the presidency. Bentsen was ready with a brutal put down. "Senator," he said shaking his head almost sadly, "I served with Jack Kennedy. I knew Jack Kennedy. Jack Kennedy was a friend of mine. Senator, you're no Jack Kennedy." The politically savvy crowd at the old theater in downtown Omaha, Nebraska, exploded with a collective gasp. The exchange was repeated over and over on news shows for the rest of the campaign. It cemented Quayle's public image as a shallow, dumb, and inexperienced politician. The Doonesbury cartoon strip portrayed him as a feather. Quayle was doomed to campaign in the back roads and small towns of America, in safe Republican territory where Bush's handlers thought he could do the least amount of damage to the ticket.

Quayle in 1992

Despite a concerted effort to improve his public image during Bush's first term, Quayle's standing with the public stayed about the same. In 1992, he once again became the target of ridicule when he took on Murphy Brown, a television situation comedy character, for deciding to have a baby out of wedlock. A worse moment, however, came in June at a spelling bee in New Jersey. As a little boy wrote the word potato on a blackboard, Quayle helpfully leaned forward and urged him to put the letter "E" on the end. Quayle's spelling goof reinforced every negative impression many voters had of him as a not-very-bright lightweight. Some Republicans urged Bush to replace Quayle, but Bush refused.

CLINTON'S CHOICE FOR VICE PRESIDENT: AL GORE

Clinton had enough problems without complicating matters by picking a controversial vice presidential candidate. The selection of a running mate is the first presidential level decision that is made by a presidential nominee. It is closely scrutinized for evidence of the candidate's judgment and ability to make major decisions. So Clinton and his staff followed a careful selection process, similar to the one used by Dukakis four years before to

The week after the Democratic National Convention, Diane Sawyer of ABC New "Prime Time Live" interviewed Democratic vice presidential candidate Al Gore and his wife Tipper at their farm in Carthage, Tennessee. (Photo by Steve Fenn, Capital Cities/ABC Inc.)

settle upon Bentsen. The process included extensive background checks to make sure that the person chosen was not hiding anything embarrassing.

From the beginning, it seemed likely that Clinton would look for a running mate with Washington experience because as the governor of a small state he had not held federal office in Washington. He and his advisers debated the wisdom of picking someone older who would offset Clinton's youth or picking someone younger who would reinforce Clinton's slowly emerging public image as a youthful innovator. They decided to go with the reinforcing choice. What sealed the choice was a private meeting between Clinton and Gore late one night at a Washington hotel. They did not know one another very well, although both were members of the Democratic Leadership Council, the group started by moderate Southern Democrats to steer the national Democratic party back towards the middle. Some Clinton staffers feared that the two might not get along because they were natural rivals. Both were smart, ambitious, Southern politicians of about the same age who wanted to be president. But Clinton and Gore hit it off almost instantly. The selection of Gore, a fellow baby boomer, fellow Southerner, and someone who liked talking about policy as much as Clinton did was widely viewed as an enormous boost to the Democratic ticket.

Al Gore

Gore, the son of a former U.S. senator, had grown up in Washington, attended Ivy League Schools, and, as his father, Albert, Sr., said, been bred for national office. He had sought the presidency himself four years earlier when he was only 40 years old, but his own presidential campaign never gained much traction. Gore brought many pluses to the Clinton campaign. He had earned a reputation in the Senate as a staunch environmentalist, a record that would help offset concerns about Clinton's record in Arkansas. He was also a devoted family man, a characteristic thought to be a plus for a ticket headed by a candidate who had admitted he had some problems in the past with his own marriage.

All of this meant that Gore was ready for prime time. The differences between Gore's first solo trip as a vice presidential candidate and that of Quayle four years earlier could not have been more stark. His experience as a member of Congress, senator, and 1988 presidential candidate had significantly reduced the start-up time for a new candidacy. He hit the ground running. Gore got off to a quicker start than Bentsen had four years earlier. Bentsen was a little out of practice as a candidate because he had not had a tough reelection fight in Texas in years.

Gore not only had the qualifications and experience on paper for the job, but the personal trauma of almost losing his only son had also changed his demeanor, for the better. Gore had been notoriously stiff in public. (There was even a joke about it: How do you tell the difference between Al Gore and a Secret Service Agent? Gore is the stiff one. Gore still told that joke on himself four years later.) Although Gore still had the extraordinary discipline to keep every hair in place while everyone else wilted in the humidity of a hot summer day, his feelings rode much closer to the surface in 1992. His son's near death had triggered an internal change that made him a more open and candid person and made him a more compelling public figure because he could connect with people better. He was much more likely to speak his mind as a result, and this ability was an advantage in a year when voters wanted candor from their politicians.

During an interview at the Philadelphia airport in late July, he spoke about how his son's tragedy had changed his life.

> People go through a lot of changes in their lives, and the last four years have been a time of great many changes in my life. I set my priorities in a completely different way now than I did then. (His son's accident) . . . was a real turning point in my life, and I just began to look at life very differently after that. It's a lot more fun to be focused on something that is a lot larger than the campaign itself. The dialogue in this campaign is a means to an end and not an end in itself. My role in it is something that I have in perspective. It's about more than Bill Clinton and me. It's about more than the election.

Gore began to emerge as a kind of co-president, a peer rather than a junior partner relegated to a traditional supporting role representing the United States at the funerals of foreign heads of state. Clinton said that if he was elected, Gore would be the chief liaison to Congress and take particular responsibility for environmental issues. Jimmy Carter was the first president to treat his vice president, Walter Mondale, as a partner in the administration. Mondale had an office near the Oval Office. Bush also had his share of responsibility during the Reagan presidency. Even Quayle had a special role in the Bush administration. He not only acted as the conservative point man in the White House, the person who would push for the conservative agenda, but he also headed up the White House Competitiveness Council, which reversed environmental regulations for business interests.

In a pattern that would be repeated during the Clinton presidency, Clinton and Gore campaigned together frequently during the general election campaign, far more often than was usual. Accompanied by their wives Hillary and Tipper, they took bus tours that became a symbol of the campaign's efforts to reach the public. Their relationship grew closer as they spent hours talking and bumping along in the bus. Bush, by contrast, rarely appeared in public with Quayle.

JAMES STOCKDALE

The third major vice presidential candidate made one disastrous public appearance that demonstrated once and for all the importance and significance of the position of second banana. James Bond Stockdale, a retired vice admiral from the U.S. Navy, who had been the highest ranking American officer held in a prisoner of war camp in North Vietnam during the Vietnam War, was the reluctant vice presidential candidate in 1992, the running mate of H. Ross Perot, the independent presidential candidate. (See Chapter 9, Perotmania.) In the spring as Perot's supporters scrambled to get Perot's name on the ballot in all 50 states, they discovered that he needed to have a running mate to meet the conditions for ballot access in certain states. As a short-term measure, Perot picked Stockdale, a man he admired greatly who had won the Medal of Honor for his heroic military service.

Stockdale himself would be the first person to say that he was not suited to be a vice presidential candidate. He was not a politician. He was also 68 years old and suffered from the lingering effects of his imprisonment and torture. Perot intended to replace his interim choice with a more appropriate vice presidential candidate later in the summer, perhaps in time for a convention he proposed to hold for himself, but long before that took place, Perot abruptly quit the race. When Perot just as suddenly leapt back into the race on October 1, it was too late to substitute Stockdale for someone else. It may not have mattered except that the vice presidential candidates were scheduled to debate just two weeks later on October 13 in Atlanta.

Stockdale's Background

Stockdale was a genuine American hero. He was born in Illinois, the son of a potter. Stockdale graduated from the Naval Academy and served in active duty in the Navy for 37 years. For most of that time, he served at sea as a fighter pilot aboard aircraft carriers. Navy fighter pilots are among the most daring and skilled in the U.S. military because they are required to land their planes on aircraft carriers on heaving, heavy seas. During his second tour of combat in Vietnam, his A-4 jet was shot down over North Vietnam. He parachuted directly into the middle of a crowd of North Vietnamese who beat him badly. His leg was also crushed in the fall. It was broken a second time during captivity and never healed properly so years later he still walked with a pronounced limp. Because he was the highest ranking military officer in captivity, he was subjected to hair-raising torture. He once slashed his own wrists with broken glass after a torture session to show his captors that he would rather die than tell any secrets and betray his country.

Stockdale had many admirers of his heroic past, including Orson Swindle who headed up Perot's grassroots organization of volunteers called United We Stand. When Perot got back into the presidential race in late September, Swindle acted as the chief spokesman for the campaign. Like Stockdale, Swindle had been a career military man who had been taken prisoner during the Vietnam War. He met Stockdale while imprisoned at the notorious Hanoi Hilton, the big POW camp in North Vietnam, after he was captured in 1966. Stockdale had been seized about a year earlier. He vividly recalled that his first sight of Stockdale was of his bright, steely blue eyes, which he glimpsed through the wooden slats of his cell. The prisoners were held in separate cells and communicated by tapping out coded messages to one another. He credited Stockdale with saving his life.

He was eager to talk about Stockdale in Dallas just four days before the big vice presidential debate. Swindle's recollections of Stockdale provided some insight into the extraordinary loyalty and admiration he inspired.

> I met him by whispering under the door to him. I never saw his face until six years later. When he moved into the cell block, I was very demoralized. I had been worked over very badly and had written a confession and all the typical propaganda crap that they put you through after they tortured the hell out of you. I felt very badly about it. I thought I was the only one who was weak and had betrayed my country. He had an amazing effect on me. He was an inspiration. I give him credit for me being sane and probably alive. He was a rock of Gibraltar. No leader is tested like a leader in prison. It's a bizarre world. Every logical course of action leads to abuse and punishment and perhaps death. He was just an inspiration.

While no one disputed Stockdale's courage, patriotism, and intellect, he had no experience in the rough and tumble world of politics. To outsiders, politics sometimes looks easy, but politics entails specific skills and experiences just like any other profession. For the past ten years, Stockdale had been living the quiet peaceful life of a contemplative intellectual. He was a senior

Chris Wallace, a correspondent for "PrimeTime Live," an ABC news show, interviewed Vice President Dan Quayle and his wife Marilyn in late August at the vice president's residence in Washington. (Photo by Terry Ashe, Capital Cities/ABC Inc.)

research fellow at the Hoover Institution at Stanford University. He spent his time thinking and writing. He was writing a book about the Greek stoic philosopher, Epictetus, a man who like Stockdale himself had been imprisoned and crippled. John Bunzel, an associate of Stockdale's and great admirer, worried aloud before the debate that the political exercise would humiliate or trivialize this great man. "If you drew up a list of people one million names long to be vice president, you would never think of him," he said.

THE VICE PRESIDENTIAL DEBATE

Bunzel's worst fears were realized from the opening moment of the vice presidential candidate debate in Atlanta. "Who am I and why am I here?" blurted Stockdale. The line was supposed to be funny because millions of Americans flicked on their television sets that night and saw Stockdale for the very first time. Most knew who Gore and Quayle were. These voters were all saying to themselves who is that guy? But instead of coming across as humorous, Stockdale sounded like a confused old man who genuinely did not know why he was there. The debate deteriorated from that point on for Stockdale.

Expectations for the Vice Presidential Debate

The press and the pundits had set the expectations for the debate performance very high for Gore because he was a skilled and polished public performer. Expectations for Quayle, gaffe-prone during his term as vice president, were low, and expectations for Stockdale were also low. All Stockdale had to do was answer a few questions and appear reasonably alert to pass the minimal muster required of him.

Gore was so practiced that he was criticized for being wooden and too rigid. He scrupulously kept to the script of talking points that campaign strategists had agreed to in advance. He repeatedly blamed the Bush administration for the country's economic malaise. Afterwards, Gore was criticized by some Democrats for not defending Clinton against the repeated attacks of Quayle. Responding to Quayle, however, was a no-win situation for Gore as he was coached to refuse to rise to any bait dangled by Quayle that would get Gore off the economic message he was supposed to communicate during the debate.

Quayle did better than expected but that was not difficult. All the bad publicity that Quayle had received during the previous four years had given him the public image of a man who could not spell potato. But he did far better than anticipated. He took on the time honored vice presidential role of attack dog and aggressively criticized Clinton for lacking integrity. "Bill Clinton has trouble telling the truth," he said over and over again. "This is a fundamental problem with Bill Clinton: trust and character. . . . Bill Clinton has trouble telling the truth."

Stockdale seemed lost on the stage. At one point, he had to ask Hal Bruno, the moderator, to repeat a question because he had turned off his hearing aid. Every once in awhile, he pulled himself together and got off a good line. As Quayle and Gore snapped at one another, Stockdale quipped, "Now I see why America is in gridlock." At another point, he complained that he felt like an observer at a ping-pong game. But overall, Stockdale gave such a bad debate performance that even the most loyal Perot supporters, the Perot volunteers who staffed the telephone bank in Dallas at campaign headquarters, were stunned. The volunteers held a debate watch party with pizza and soft drinks. They watched the 90-minute debate on live television in stunned silence. They were struck dumb with horror.

Stockdale's inability to answer basic public policy questions as well as his generally disoriented demeanor was thought to hurt Perot and stall any momentum that may have been developing for Perot after the first presidential debate, which had taken place two nights earlier in St. Louis. Stockdale was unable to answer a question on health care financing, a major concern of voters, pleading, "I'm out of ammunition on this." He also must have come across to many Americans who knew nothing about his background as a bit strange when he described how "I ran a civilization for a few years." He was referring to his leadership role in the POW camp, but many viewers did not know that. Only 2 percent of the viewers surveyed by ABC News thought that Stockdale had "won" the debate.

All vice presidential candidates must cross a threshold of credibility. Voters need to be able to see them as potential presidents if the worst should happen and the president is unable to complete his term. No one could conclude from his debate performance that Stockdale could take over the presidency in an emergency. His wife Sybil described the debate as a "gruesome process" the next day. She compared the debate to "throwing Christians to the lions in ancient Rome." Much later it was learned that Stockdale had suffered a stroke some time earlier. While anyone unaccustomed to television lights and public speaking might become disoriented on national television for the first time, the stroke also helped to explain his halting performance.

The upshot of all the debate analysis was that Quayle may have won the battle but Gore won the war. Quayle fulfilled his mission by attacking Bill Clinton, but the pit bull performance did nothing to erase voter reservations about his ability to serve as president. At times, the combative Quayle seemed out of control. By contrast, Gore was the winner because he came across as the most presidential candidate even though some people thought he was too wooden and stiff. The befuddled Stockdale was so obviously unsuited to be a heartbeat away from the presidency that he and his ticket lost badly. After the debate, Stockdale disappeared from public view and did not campaign again. Eventually, many Perot voters casted a vote for Perot as a protest with little expectation that he would be elected president. To these voters, Stockdale's ability to hold the office of vice president was irrelevant.

In 1992, the vice president remained very much a secondary consideration to voters who understandably were more concerned about the ability and vision of the presidential candidates. But the campaign showed once again the strengths and weaknesses of the candidates for the number two spots. While many citizens seemed indifferent to the vice presidency, history has shown many times that the vice president may need to take over the presidency without notice. This campaign allowed the public to make an informed assessment about the second banana who might some day be president.

Chapter 10

Winning and Losing: The November Election

On the first Tuesday in November, more than 104 million men and women in the United States went to a local fire station, school cafeteria, or some other public building to vote for a president. This event is the greatest exercise of democracy in the world. On this day, the vote of every single citizen counts. The vote of the wealthiest business baron on Wall Street is worth the same as that of the poorest pauper in a southern California barrio. Each voter makes a private and personal decision and records it by marking a paper ballot, pulling a lever on a voting machine, or punching a card. On November 3, 1992, the American people expressed their combined will through the individual act of voting.

THE LARGE VOTER TURNOUT

Throughout the day, reports of a larger than expected turnout filtered into the Washington, Little Rock, and Dallas command centers of the three major presidential candidates. Voters in Boston waited in line for hours. One voting machine in Indiana broke from overuse. A Clinton campaign operative in Ohio secured a court order to keep the polls open after the official closing hour so the hundreds of citizens still waiting in line could vote. In the tiny town of Kevin, Montana, 152 of the 153 registered voters got to the polls. Despite a relentless rain that pounded the Windy City all day long, turnout in Chicago reached the highest level in recent memory.

In the end, voter turnout—the number of citizens over the age of 18 who were eligible to vote and did so—was the highest recorded in 20 years, reversing a 30-year trend that may have bottomed out in 1988 when fewer than 50 percent of the registered voters bothered to participate in the presidential election. For the first time in American history, more than 100 million people had voted in a single election. As many political observers suspected throughout the day, this larger than expected turnout signaled very bad news for George Bush. Voters do not stir themselves from their routine to ratify the status quo. Indeed, in a year in which "change" was the watchword, three out of every five voters cast a ballot against the incumbent president. A total 43 percent voted for Bill Clinton and 19 percent for Ross Perot. George Bush pulled only 38 percent of the vote, a number that approximated the Republican base vote.

Voters also elected four new women to the male-dominated U.S. Senate: Carol Moseley Braun of Illinois, Dianne Feinstein and Barbara Boxer of California, and Patty Murray of Washington state. More than 100 new members won election to the U.S. House including a record number of women and minority group members.

Perot did better than any third party candidate in 80 years by pulling 19 percent of the vote on election day after a 33-day campaign run from television studios. (Photo by Cable News Network, Inc., All Rights Reserved.)

And in 14 states including California, Florida, Michigan, and Ohio, voters approved citizen initiatives—laws proposed and ratified by the people at the ballot box—imposing limits on the number of terms their members of Congress could serve.

THE ELECTORAL COLLEGE

Bill Clinton claimed victory but not because he drew 17 million more votes than Bush. He won because he carried the electoral college. To be elected president, a candidate must capture at least 270 of the 538 electoral college votes. Clinton captured 32 states and the District of Columbia to win 370 electoral college votes to Bush's 18 states and 168 electors. Perot did not carry a single state, and so he did not receive any Electoral College votes.

The electoral college may sound like some sort of institution of higher education for politicos. In fact, it is an arcane institution that comes into being once every four years for the sole purpose of electing the president. In a democracy, the candidate who receives the most votes wins, but in the United States, it is possible for a presidential candidate to win more popular votes than any other candidate and still lose the election. That is because the people do not vote directly for the president. They vote instead for presidential electors. The electors meet at each state capital a month after the election in December for a formal ceremony to actually vote for the president. In many states, the electors wear top hats, morning coats, and formal dress for this auspicious occasion. Each state dispatches the official results to Washington for an announcement on January 6 at a joint session of Congress led by the vice president, the presiding officer in the Senate. It fell to Vice President Dan Quayle, the bottom half of the losing ticket, to announce the victory of Bill Clinton and Al Gore in 1993.

Origins of the Electoral College

Democracy was a very new idea back in the 1780s when the nation's founding fathers were trying to figure out a structure for the new government. They did not want a king. They had just finished fighting a revolution for independence against King George

III of England, but they were equally leery of the prospect of mob rule and direct election of a president. In the earliest days of the republic, only men who owned property and paid taxes were even eligible to vote. Participants at the first Constitutional Conventions argued at length about how to equalize the power between large and small states and in the end came up with the electoral college as a compromise.

Under this system, each state is allocated electoral votes equal to its number of senators and representatives in Congress. While every state regardless of size sends two U.S. senators to Washington, the number of representatives is determined by population. Every 10 years, the 435 seats in the U.S. House are divvied up or reapportioned on the basis of the results of the U.S. census. As the population of the nation shifts, the power in Congress shifts right along with it. That is why the growth of population in California and the Southwest has given that state and region more clout in the U.S. House than that of New England where the population growth has been relatively lower. There are approximately half a million residents in every House district. Little Vermont up in the northwest corner of New England has a population of only half a million people so it sends only one representative to the House. Like all states, Vermont has two senators so the state gets three electoral college votes. The District of Columbia is not a state and has no senators in Congress, but it does have three times the population of Vermont so it also has three electoral college votes. California, the largest state, sends a delegation of 52 House members to Washington along with two senators—in 1993 both were women for the first time in history—so it has 54 electoral college votes.

The winner-take-all system devised by the founding fathers gives all of the state's electoral college votes to the candidate who wins the plurality of the votes in the state. In most cases, the candidate who wins the most popular votes also wins the most electoral college votes, but not always. Three times in American history, in the elections of John Quincy Adams in 1824, Rutherford B. Hayes in 1876, and Benjamin Harrison in 1888, the president actually lost the popular vote but carried enough states to win the electoral college. Back in June when Perot, Bush, and Clinton were splitting the vote fairly evenly, there was speculation that the candidates might end up dividing the vote so that no single candidate would win a majority of the electoral college. When this happens, the election is decided by the U.S. House of Representatives.

Targeting Electoral Votes

Because voters were so angry with Congress in 1992, this sort of scenario would undoubtedly have prompted demands for the elimination of the electoral college. Although Perot did better than expected in the popular vote and probably kept Clinton from getting a majority of the popular vote, Clinton won a landslide victory in the electoral college. This victory was because of the success of the Clinton campaign's strategy of targeting virtually all of its resources to the states needed to win an electoral college majority. Clinton and his campaign staff almost ignored the states that he did not expect to win. In the states he needed to win, however, his campaign spent more money on television advertising than the candidates for governor and U.S. senator in those states. This targeting strategy allowed the Clinton-Gore campaign to get the biggest bang for its bucks. Because George Bush was so far behind in so many different places, he was obliged to spend most of his advertising money on national network advertising, which is more expensive and goes to places that he has no chance at all of winning.

Throughout the general election campaign, a lot of attention is paid to national public opinion polls that record the horse race. Throughout the campaign, Clinton maintained a steady lead over Bush. The race began to tighten up during the final 10 days, a normal occurrence in national campaigns. This tightening was misleading because the real race takes place in 50 different states and the District of Columbia. The real contest is for the electoral college majority and Clinton maintained double digit leads in enough states needed to win even as his lead in the national horse race figure shrunk. It became clear to students of the electoral college that Bush had the barest chance of victory in the final week of the campaign because he was too far behind in too many different states. At that point, Bush not only needed to surge forward in many states at the same time, he also needed the Clinton campaign to collapse simultaneously in those states.

CAMPAIGN STRATEGY IN 1992

Campaign strategists have often been compared to crusty old generals who tend to learn too well the lessons of the last war and refight that war instead of recognizing the differences in a new campaign. While experience counts for a lot in a political campaign, each campaign is unique. The Bush strategists attempted to re-run the 1988 campaign when Bush beat Michael Dukakis by casting him as a risky and unreliable liberal who could not be trusted to protect the taxpayers' pocketbooks or the national security. Bill Clinton was not Michael Dukakis. The Clinton-Gore campaign was painfully aware of the price paid by Dukakis for his turn-the-other-cheek posture in 1988. Dukakis had made a mistake in ignoring Bush's attacks on his character and record and not responding to those attacks until it was too late. The Democrats learned that negative attacks stick and become accepted as the truth unless they are neutralized right away with a response.

Dukakis had also failed to deliver a compelling case for change in 1988 and allowed himself to become the central issue of the campaign. The Clinton strategists were determined to avoid this pitfall, and so they set up a 24-hour war room in the Little Rock campaign headquarters in the old *Arkansas Gazette* newspaper building. James Carville, a senior campaign strategist from Louisiana who was known as the Ragin' Cajun, hung a sign in the room that said, "The Economy, Stupid" to remind everyone to keep focused on the most important issue of the campaign. The rapid-response team remained fire engine ready 24 hours a day to give timely responses to Bush campaign attacks and to counterattack. The goal was to respond to an attack within minutes or at the most hours so that the news accounts of the charge would also contain the response and parry.

The unit became an elite within the campaign structure. It was made up of about 30 young campaign workers who were chosen for their speed and ability to think clearly and act decisively. They represented each department of the campaign (including research, press, and field) to not only draw upon the expertise in each department but also to keep their colleagues aware of the tactics of the Bush campaign. The war-room workers monitored the wire services and television and radio broadcasts. They accepted telephone calls from campaign workers in other parts of the country reporting mini-attacks in particular states and cities. They responded to the daily "Attack Fax" from the Bush campaign. (The Bush campaign used the facsimile machine to send off daily diatribes against Clinton to newspapers and local Bush campaign offices. They were usually written by Mary Matalin, the deputy campaign manager who happened to be James Carville's girl friend, a relationship that prompted much notice during the election.) The rapid-response team was so quick on the draw that the *New York Times* canceled the Clinton campaign's subscription to its wire service after a campaign worker critiqued an article written by Gwen Ifill, the *Times'* reporter covering the Clinton campaign, right after it moved on the wire but hours before the newspaper hit the streets of New York.

The Use of Technology

Technological advances had sped up the transfer of information in every facet of American life and business including politics. Cellular telephones were standard equipment for campaign aides and journalists. When the campaign planes touched down at an airport runway, it was not unusual for a dozen or more reporters and television producers to begin dialing their offices all at once to report the latest development from the campaign trail. Reporters filed their dispatches to their editors on telephone lines from laptop computers. The network television crews routinely would broadcast live from the road bringing campaign events to voters instantly. C-Span broadcasted entire press conferences and campaign speeches each night from the campaign trail so that voters with the time to watch could see and judge for themselves. Facsimiles became an integral part of every campaign operation. All of the campaigns faxed out press releases and statements almost nonstop throughout the day.

The Clinton Campaign and Technology

The Clinton campaign developed the most sophisticated communications system in a year of unusual technological innovation in political campaigns. The Clinton campaign gave a high-tech gloss to the grittiest part of political campaigning, the field operation. Field is the blue-collar sector of political campaigns. Field organizers, usually young, idealistic, eager, and poorly paid, are the "grunts" on a campaign staff. They set up shop in local communities and are responsible for tailoring the candidate's message for local consumption. Because radio and television has become a major source of information about political campaigns for most voters, the Clinton field staff became communications specialists in 1992. They turned GOTV, the age-old field practice of identifying voters and getting them to the polls, from Get Out The Vote to Get On TV. Like their counterparts in the war room in Little Rock, the field operatives primary mission was to deflect and respond to Republican attacks and get out the Clinton campaign message to voters in their area. Instead of being organized by congressional district, the traditional way to divide up the field, the Clinton-Gore organizers were organized by media markets. A media market is the geographic area that falls within the transmission signal of television and radio stations.

Every state office had a computer that could communicate with the campaign headquarters in Little Rock, a facsimile machine, and radio actuality equipment. Radio actuality equipment enabled the field workers to provide local radio stations with usable sound bites from the campaign. The local campaign workers tried to get popular local officials who supported Clinton to make statements for the campaign. A statement from George Stephanopoulos, the campaign communications director, could be relayed by electronic mail called E-mail to every single campaign office within eight minutes. This set up helped to ensure that the entire sprawling campaign staff would sing from the same hymnal and deliver the same Clinton-Gore message. Elaine Guiney, the Massachusetts state director for the Clinton campaign, complained that she got so much E-mail from Little Rock that she did not have time to read it during the day. She took her messages home to read them each night.

The collapse of the old coalition that served the Democratic party so well from the time of Franklin Roosevelt until the time of the Republican ascendancy with Nixon's election in 1968 meant that the Democrats had to put as much effort in voter persuasion as voter contact. On a given day 200 to 300 different spokesmen for

Clinton-Gore scattered in media markets across the country might be giving the same Clinton message in the same way. The campaign coordinated the field message with the message being conveyed by Clinton on the stump and by the paid advertising.

Voter Contact Programs

The Clinton-Gore campaign also developed a voter-contact program to respond to the heightened demand from voters for more specific information on policy positions and a desire to feel involved in the political process. The program called "Americans for Change" was designed to not only identify supporters but to make them feel invested in the process and empowered. The voter-contact program was one more manifestation of the use of new ways to make voters feel reconnected to their political process. The first part of the program was the Sign-Up Campaign, a simple volunteer card distributed at Clinton and Gore campaign rallies. The field organizers collected the cards after each rally and later would telephone the volunteers and give them tasks. The sign-up card carried an 800 number for those too eager to wait for a call. It was 1-800-FOR-BILL. Phase two was called 10 More for Clinton-Gore, a way for supporters to recruit 10 friends at the health club, at work, and at volunteer activities without having to spend time at a phone bank calling strangers or going door to door in an unfamiliar neighborhood. The final phase was called the Doorstep Campaign for supporters to recruit their neighbors in an old-fashioned door-to-door recruitment drive.

DEMOCRATIC SYSTEM IN THE U.S. IN CRISIS

When communism crumbled in the former U.S.S.R. and Eastern Europe, the residents of those countries began a steady march towards democracy. But while the rest of the world seemed to be going towards democracy, the world's oldest democracy seemed to be doing the opposite. After the 1988 presidential campaign, the John and Mary R. Markle Foundation, a charitable foundation devoted to the study of mass communications in democracy, commissioned a study to examine the role of citizens, candidates, and the media to try and determine what had gone awry. The commission report grimly concluded that widespread public cynicism, voter ignorance, and low election turnout threatened the American democratic process. The report identified "citizen abdication of the electoral process" as the single most disturbing finding. The average person was walking away from responsibilities as a citizen and didn't seem to care or understand that this attitude was putting the entire system at risk.

"Our democratic ideals suggest that the media, the candidates, and the voters should interact in a kind of 'golden triangle' of reason and responsibility," the report said. "The role of the media is to inform and protect the electorate against misrepresentation; the role of the candidates is to inform and inspire the electorate; the role of the voters is to educate themselves for the task of making judicious choices."

The commission found that this golden triangle had collapsed because the media, the candidates, and the voters had fallen down on the job. "American voters today do not seem to understand their rightful place in the operation of American democracy," said the report. "They act as if they believe that presidential elections belong to somebody else, most notably presidential candidates and their handlers." Voters were indifferent and ignorant and did not bother to learn the most basic things about the candidates and the issues. The commission also blamed the candidates and the media. The candidates delivered superficial messages that were designed to manipulate rather than educate it said. The media was criticized for devoting most of its time to covering "the election as a competition and the personalities of the contestants rather than with the substance of the public agenda." In other words, reporters spent more time saying who was ahead and who was behind than telling voters what the candidates were saying and what they wanted to do if elected.

SEEDS OF CHANGE IN 1992

A number of factors combined to improve this bleak assessment during the 1992 campaign. Dramatic changes that had been taking place in the U.S. economy for more than 10 years finally reached a certain critical mass so that many workers permanently lost their high-paying manufacturing jobs and were being forced into lower-paying positions in the service economy. In other words, a factory worker making more than $10 an hour plus benefits in a union shop producing a product would find himself flipping hamburgers in a fast-food outlet for half that amount and no benefits. This problem not only hit the blue-collar factory workers in the Rust Belt states like Michigan where the auto industry had been struggling against foreign competition for years, but it also hit the white-collar workers in the high-technology industries in places like California and Massachusetts. The economic distress was so widespread that it created tremendous anxiety even among workers who still had their jobs. Polls showed that a clear majority of citizens thought the country was heading in the wrong direction.

The conservative social agenda of the radical right that enjoyed such preeminence during the Reagan and Bush years had reached a point where it was generating an enormous backlash, particularly among professional women, young people, and supporters of abortion rights. Presidents Reagan and Bush appointed conservative justices to the Supreme Court whose rulings were beginning to chip away at the decision, Roe v. Wade, which had legalized abortion. Many voters, particularly working women, had also become politicized by the confirmation hearings of Supreme Court Justice Clarence Thomas in 1991. Anita Hill, a law school professor, accused Thomas of sexually harassing her years before when he had been her boss at a federal agency. At first, the Senate Judiciary Committee, which had no female members, did not take the complaint seriously. When the committee held public hearings, some of the Republican senators on the panel questioned Hill so sharply that many viewers felt she was being victimized a second time in order to save Thomas' appointment. Anita Hill became a rallying cry for millions of angry women.

At the same time, the first wave of the enormous baby boom generation, the largest population group in the United States, was approaching middle-age and becoming increasingly concerned about the condition of the world in which their children were growing up. Dozens of studies had found that the rich got richer and the poor poorer during the 1980s. Opportunities for reaching and maintaining a middle-class lifestyle also shrunk dramatically.

Many parents could not afford to send their children to college. They also could not afford to provide long-term medical and nursing home care for their aging parents. Young couples could not afford to buy their own homes. Millions of families did not have health insurance even though they worked full time.

All of these factors rested like a firecracker underneath the body politic just waiting to explode. Throughout the campaign year, reporters frequently came across volunteer campaign workers who confessed that they were getting involved in a campaign for the first time or for the first time since the 1970s because they were just so mad or worried or fed up. From the snows of New Hampshire to sunny southern California, voters were in a demanding mood wanting real answers and candor from the candidates for president. Paul Tsongas was the first candidate to describe the situation. On the first page of his "A Call to Economic Arms", he wrote:

America faces great economic peril as our standard of living is threatened by Europe 1992 and the Pacific Rim. Once the world's greatest economic power, we are selling off our national patrimony as we sink ever deeper into national debt. The Reagan-Bush years have seen us become the world's greatest debtor nation. America is also witnessing the weakening of its social fabric as more and more families dissolve under the onslaught of a culture that glorifies the immediate and the shallow. As our historic values are disregarded by today's society-in-a-hurry, the civility of America has been lessened. Finally, America is adrift as our leaders flinch from the difficult decisions that will safeguard us from the energy and environmental threats that confront us. This nation's will is not being called upon on the home front because of a fear that our people are not ready for an honest and forceful response to these threats. I strongly disagree.

He was correct that many people would respond to the threat and take action in 1992. The most successful candidates were those who understood that this was a year to speak the truth, confront the reality of the present, and offer some ideas for a better future. As Clinton evolved as a presidential candidate, he adopted many of the positions and tactics of his rivals, including Tsongas, Brown, and Perot. On Father's Day in late June when Clinton released his economic program called "Putting People First," he was asked about the influence of his competitors on the plan. Clinton said he liked the question and eagerly credited them with influencing his thinking. "I've learned something from all the candidates," he said while standing in a television studio in Atlanta where he had just completed a televised town meeting. "They all can say there is a bit of them in this plan." He said that Senator Bob Kerrey of Nebraska had impressed him with his health care proposals, Senator Tom Harkin of Iowa with the need for public construction projects to put people to work, former Senator Paul Tsongas with the need for economic policies that encourage greater investment by business, and former Governor Jerry Brown on the vital importance of political reform. For all the criticism Clinton received for being "Slick Willie" and difficult to pin down at times, it was this sort of candor that many voters found reassuring.

"I just think that the system doesn't work for most people and when it doesn't you can't keep democracy alive," he said summarizing the reasons for the undercurrent of frustration and anger in the electorate. "I'm not just selling a plan. I'm selling an idea. I've got to make the American people believe this plan is the instrument for making government work again for all the people. That is what I want them to believe. That we can make this thing work. We can do better."

BUSH'S EVOLVING CAMPAIGN STRATEGY

President Bush tried to do what he had done so successfully in 1988. He tried to make Clinton and his character the central issue of the campaign and scare voters into voting against Clinton. At the same time, he tried to maximize the advantages of his experience and age. After seven consecutive presidents from the World War II generation, the nation had become accustomed to looking to those of Bush's generation for leadership. But 1992 was different from 1988 in part because Bush was the president now and his record and performance were also being assessed by the voters.

After Secretary of State James Baker, Bush's longtime close friend from Texas, resigned his position as head of the nation's foreign policy apparatus to return to the White House and effectively run the Bush reelection campaign from there in late August, the Bush campaign came up with a new strategy to use the president's incumbency to full avail. "Every time the public sees him acting as the president, then it's good for him politically," said Robert Teeter, Bush's campaign manager. Hurricane Andrew

After a hard fought campaign in which the candidates attacked one another, a lot of voters might have shared Dan Wasserman's view of the three major candidates. (Cartoon by Dan Wasserman, *Boston Globe*, distributed by LA Times Syndicate.)

quickly showed how a president can be both helped and hurt by that sort of Rose Garden strategy.

The Federal Emergency Management Administration (FEMA), a small federal agency that had become a dumping ground for political appointees during the Reagan and Bush administrations, came under heavy fire for botching the clean-up efforts in areas devastated by the hurricane in southern Florida and Louisiana. With Baker back in the White House, the administration moved quickly to put Transportation Secretary Andrew H. Card, a former state representative from Massachusetts, in charge of the clean-up efforts. Card, as a member of the president's cabinet, had the power and authority to coordinate and speed-up the federal clean-up efforts.

The Santa Claus Tour

Bush then began what became known as the Santa Claus tour to deliver federal largesse in person to key states. He flew to southern Florida and promised to provide millions of dollars in federal assistance as well as to rebuild the Homestead Air Force Base that had been destroyed in the storm. Homestead had been slated for closure even before Hurricane Andrew hit, and Defense Department officials among others said that there was no military justification for rebuilding it. He went to Carswell Air Force Base in Texas and announced that he was authorizing the $4 billion sale of 150 F-16 fighter jets to Taiwan. The announcement represented a change in position. The jets were manufactured at a General Dynamics plant in Fort Worth. General Dynamics had said that it would be forced to layoff 3,000 workers without that contract. He then went to South Dakota to hand out help to the wheat farmers, $755 million in emergency disaster aid and $1 billion for the Wheat Export Enhancement Program. The position represented another reversal of position because Bush was an advocate of free trade and opponent of trade subsidies. He went to Fredericksburg, Virginia, to sign a bill increasing loan guarantees for the Small Business Administration. He flew to St. Louis to announce approval of the sale of 72 F-15 fighter plans to Saudi Arabia, a move that saved about 7,000 jobs in the aircraft industry in Missouri. He also went to the farm states to announce that he was exempting ethanol, a fuel made from corn, from the Clean Air Act.

While the voters who were directly affected by those decisions may have been pleased, the news media carried the story of Bush's generosity to voters in every section of the country. He quickly came under fire for using federal tax dollars and Air Force One to

President Bush used the advantages of his office to do favors for voters in key states. (Cartoon by Dan Wasserman, *Boston Globe*, distributed by LA Times Syndicate.)

buy votes. The political press noted that this largesse was going to critical swing states or must-win states. "There were no reindeer pulling the Bush motorcade across the Farm Belt today, but the people here still might have thought they were getting a visit from Santa Claus, " said Brit Hume, the White House correspondent for ABC News, in a report from the Midwest one night in September.

The Failure of the Character Issue

When giveaways didn't seem to be working, Bush shifted gears to draw a distinction between himself and Clinton on character and by casting Arkansas as a pathetic backwater. He had done much the same thing in 1988 with a strategy of painting Democratic nominee Michael Dukakis as a risky liberal and Dukakis' home state of Massachusetts as a safe harbor for criminals, polluters, and high taxes. While Bush admitted that he voted for Thomas Dewey, the Republican presidential nominee running against President Harry Truman in the 1948 presidential election (when Bill Clinton was only two years old), he cast himself as the candidate in Truman's tradition in 1992. "Truman was a man of decisiveness, not equivocation," said Bush while campaigning in Wisconsin. "He'd find little in common with Governor Clinton, a man who hedges or ducks on almost every tough issue."

Arkansas has always been among the nation's poorest states with a high welfare rate and low literacy rate. At the beginning of September, the Bush campaign issued a five-page paper on the "Little Rock of Horrors," that detailed every tax hike ever approved by Governor Clinton during his 12 years in office. Bush campaigned one day in the six states that surround Arkansas in a series of tarmac appearances accusing Clinton of being "Governor Taxes" and lax on crime and being the steward of a state with polluted streams and poor public education. The point of all this name calling was to scare people into voting against Clinton. During a bus tour of Georgia, Vice President Quayle warned that Clinton's proposals would cost Georgia 75,000 jobs because Clinton would cut defense spending and raise taxes.

Bush's rhetoric got nastier and more personal as election day approached. Conservative Republican House members began to suggest that Clinton was some kind of secret socialist who had

President Bush tried old-fashioned train rides as a way to catch up with the front-running Democratic ticket in the fall. (Photo courtesy of the Bush Presidential Materials Project of the National Archives.)

picked up all sorts of weird ideas while studying more than 20 years earlier at Oxford University in England where he was a Rhodes scholar. Although no evidence ever emerged to dispute Clinton's claim that he traveled to Moscow on winter break simply for a vacation, Representative Bob Dornan, a conservative Democrat from California, charged that Clinton was one of a "group of radical students enamored with communism, the Soviet Union, and Ho Chi Minh." Bush soon picked up the cry. Just as Bush had jeered at Dukakis for being a "card-carrying member of the ACLU," the American Civil Liberties Union, an organization dedicated to the protection of the Bill of Rights to the U.S. Constitution, he tried to cast Clinton as a proponent of "social engineering," someone who was un-American. At the same time, the Bush campaign was trying to denigrate Clinton and his background. A Bush campaign commercial featured hillbilly music in an ad to detail the sales tax increases adopted in Arkansas during Clinton's 12 years in office.

But none of this negative campaigning seemed to make a difference with voters. Bush had little positive to say about himself or his plans for a second term. He delivered one major speech on his economic program at the Detroit Economic Club on September 10, but the proposals were largely familiar ones dressed up in new packaging called the "Agenda for American Renewal." Even then Bush pushed the issue of trust and character rather than the substance of his proposals. "The question is who can lead America to a better, freer, more prosperous and fulfilling future," he said. "Not just for us, but for the next generation, our kids and grandkids."

Bush Enters the Talk Show Game

By October Bush was desperate enough to solicit invitations from the talk television and radio shows he had disdained earlier in the

George Bush generally avoided television talk shows until the general election campaign when he was trailing Bill Clinton. Charles Gibson of "Good Morning America" on ABC interviewed the president in Washington. (Photo by Capital Cities / ABC Inc.)

year. He even granted an interview to MTV's Tabitha Soren, the "Choose or Lose" reporter, although he had flatly refused to take any questions from an audience of young people as Clinton and Gore had. On "Larry King Live" on October 7, he continued to question Clinton's trustworthiness because he said trust was what the election was all about. "Who do you trust to lead this country?" he asked Larry King. "I served this country, and I served it in uniform, and I believe I've earned the trust in that capacity from the American people. I've made tough decisions. I have not waffled; I've been on one side or the other on the war, on right-to-work laws, on spotted owls or NAFTA (North American Free Trade) agreements." He even changed his schedule to eat breakfast at a waffle house in the South to underscore his charge that Clinton was an unreliable waffler.

This strategy backfired because Bush's own trustworthiness became suspect when it was learned that Bush administration officials had tampered with private passport files to look for evidence to discredit Clinton. They even searched the files of Governor Clinton's mother, Virginia Kelley. Then an indictment of former Defense Secretary Caspar Weinberger made public the Friday before the election said that Bush had not been truthful when he denied any knowledge of the U.S.A. and Iran trading arms for hostages.

At the same time, Bush's economic record was coming under fire from both Clinton and Perot. Bush had promised to create 30 million new jobs over eight years when elected in 1988, but only 1 million had been created. The Clinton-Gore ad makers did their own version of Pat Buchanan's devastating "Read My Lips" ad which featured Bush himself promising to not raise taxes during his 1988 convention speech. "We can't afford four more years," intoned the narrator of the ad.

When a campaign is losing, it seems snakebitten and nothing goes right. Bush became increasingly agitated on the stump. At the end of the final week of campaigning, he called Clinton and Gore "two bozos." In Michigan, he said, "My dog Millie knows more about foreign affairs than these two bozos." He labeled Gore, the environmental specialist, "the ozone man . . . This guy's crazy. He is way out, far out, man."

The three presidential candidates debated on live national television three times in October of 1992 in encounters that attracted millions of viewers. (Photo courtesy of the Bush Presidential Materials Project of the National Archives.)

A successful campaign is one in which the message coming from both the paid television commercials and the unpaid news coverage are the same, or at least compatible. This agitated president calling the Democratic nominees bozos, hardly squared with the image of the sage and trustworthy and steady hand at the tiller presented in his television ads. One final Bush ad said, "In a few days, you'll be making your choice for president . . . it's a serious choice, the most important democracy asks us to make. There are many times that the president alone must make tough decisions that affect other peoples' lives. He is the commander in chief and I want you to think about that. He must have the resolve, the maturity, the moral authority to lead the nation in times of crises." But Bush was not behaving in what many people would consider a presidential manner so the message of his ads did not carry much weight.

The Clinton-Gore campaign staff had figured out a way to get under Bush's skin in September when the Bush campaign steadfastly refused to set a date for presidential debates. They dispatched field workers dressed as big chickens to Bush rallies. The chickens drove Bush to distraction and finally led the Bush campaign to make an unexpected challenge to Clinton to debate four times. The challenge caught the Clinton-Gore campaign by surprise and was one of the few moments in the general election campaign when the Bush-Quayle team had a tactical advantage.

CLINTON'S RESPONSE TO BUSH

Meanwhile, the Clinton-Gore team stuck to its issue-oriented message. A general election Clinton commercial showed clips from the Clinton-Gore bus tour. "They've called for an end to welfare as we know it," the ad said. "So welfare can be a second chance, not a way of life. They've sent a strong signal to criminals by supporting the death penalty, and they've rejected the old tax-and-spend politics. Clinton's balanced 12 budgets, and they've proposed a new plan investing in people, detailing $140 billion in spending cuts they'd make right now. Clinton-Gore. For people. For a change." In the final week, Clinton tweaked Bush by campaigning in Republican cowboy country, the states of Colorado, Wyoming, and Montana where no Democratic presidential candidate had won in 30 years. Bush was still campaigning in the once-solid Republican South trying to shore up his shaky base.

In the end the American voters feared continuation of the status quo more than Clinton. The day after Clinton won the election, Vice President Quayle paid tribute to the victors. "If he runs the country as well as he ran his campaign, we'll be alright," he said.

When the clash and clang of the campaign subsided, the presidential election showed that people can exercise their collective will through the ballot box to make peacable change in their government. The election proved that democracy works. The campaign of 1992 was a historic one because it signaled the end of 12 years of Republican control of the White House, a generational change in power, and a turnabout in the trend toward less participation in a presidential election.

For George Bush, the much-vaunted advantages of incumbency proved to be a dead weight that dragged on his candidacy at a time when people were angry with the status quo. Bush's popularity after the brief Gulf War scared off the best-known Democrats, leaving it to younger Democrats to take up the task of running against a sitting president. Bush also had to fend off a pesky challenge from within his own party from Patrick J. Buchanan. Although Buchanan, a columnist and television commentator, was viewed as a gadfly by many critics, his barbed critique of Bush's tenure in office drew the first blood. By election day, Bush was anemic and weakened and lost three out of every five votes cast.

On the Democratic side, Bill Clinton topped a field of Democrats in part because he was the best prepared for a presidential campaign. He had thought about running for president and planned for the campaign for a long time. When the time came to step up to the plate and hit the first ball, he knew exactly why he was running. He did not exactly hit a home run the first time up to bat. He won his party's nomination only after a protracted battle. But he won the game by casting himself as a new type of Democrat who was pragmatic and forward thinking. He led his political party to its first presidential victory in 16 years.

Ross Perot's candidacy stirred millions of nonpolitical citizens to political action. As a billionaire businessman who had never held public office, he personified the anti-politician mood of the public in 1992. Perot also helped to educate the electorate about the danger of deficit spending and the need for sacrifice in the short run to improve the economy in the long run.

This campaign encouraged many citizens to become involved in the political process. Some were inspired to volunteer and work for a particular candidacy because of fear: fear of losing a job or losing a civil right. Others just wanted change. The candidates attempted to bypass the press filter and speak directly to voters in 1992 to better address the concerns of the people. The media, particularly television and radio, helped educate and inform the electorate by providing new forums for the candidates on talk shows. The press also tried to better focus their coverage on more substantive issues. While some citizens remain deeply cynical and suspicious about the government, the election showed a strong belief in self-government and the democratic process when more than 100 million citizens voted on election day. In the end it seemed fitting that the election of 1992 would produce a new president who was born in a place called Hope.

Recommended Reading List

The American Heritage Pictorial History of the Presidents of the United States. Two volumes. New York: American Heritage, 1968.

Christine M. Black and Thomas Oliphant. *All By Myself: The Unmaking of a Presidential Campaign.* Chester, CT: The Globe Pequot Press, 1989.

James Bryce. *The American Commonwealth.* New York: Macmillan, 1917.

Timothy Crouse. *The Boys on the Bus: Riding with the Campaign Press Corps.* New York: Ballantine Books, 1973.

Dayton Duncan. *Grass Roots: One Year in the Life of the New Hampshire Presidential Primary.* New York: Viking, 1991.

Jack W. Germond and Jules Witcover. *Whose Broad Stripes and Bright Stars? The Trivial Pursuit of the Presidency 1988.* New York: Warner Books, 1989.

David McCullough. *Truman.* New York: Simon & Schuster, 1992.

Joe McGinniss. *The Selling of the President 1968.* New York: Trident Press, 1969.

Thomas P. (Tip) O'Neill Jr. *Man of the House: The Life and Political Memoirs of Speaker Tip O'Neill, with William Novak.* New York: Random House, 1987.

Nelson W. Polsby and Aaron Wilavsky. *Presidential Elections Strategies of American Electoral Politics,* fifth edition. New York: Charles Scribner's Sons, 1980.

Richard Reeves. *Convention.* New York: Harcourt Brace Jovanovich, 1977.

William L. Riordan. *Plunkitt of Tammany Hall.* New York: E. P. Dutton & Co., Inc., 1963.

Smithsonian Exposition Books. *Every Four Years.* New York: W. W. Norton & Co., 1980.

Dr. Hunter S. Thompson. *Fear and Loathing on the Campaign Trail '72*. San Francisco: Straight Arrow Books, 1973.

Theodore H. White. *The Making of the President 1960*. New York: Antheneum Publishers, 1961.

——. *The Making of the President 1964*. New York: Antheneum Publishers, 1965.

Jules Witcover. *Crapshoot: Rolling the Dice on the Vice Presidency*. New York: Crown Publishers, Inc., 1992.

——. *85 Days: The Last Campaign of Robert Kennedy*. New York: Putnam's, 1969.

James Wooten. *Dasher: The Roots and the Rising of Jimmy Carter*. New York: Summit Books, 1978.

Index

by Linda Webster

DATE DUE
